Bond
No.1 for exam success

MW01130386

Maths

Assessment Papers

Challenge

10–11+ years

OXFORD
UNIVERSITY PRESS

Great Clarendon Street, Oxford, OX2 6DP, United Kingdom

Oxford University Press is a department of the University of Oxford.
It furthers the University's objective of excellence in research, scholarship,
and education by publishing worldwide. Oxford is a registered trade mark
of Oxford University Press in the UK and in certain other countries

British Library Cataloguing in Publication Data
Data available

978-0-19-277829-1

10 9 8 7 6 5 4 3 2 1

Paper used in the production of this book is a natural, recyclable
product made from wood grown in sustainable forests.
The manufacturing process conforms to the environmental
regulations of the country of origin.

Printed in China

Acknowledgements

The Publishers would like to thank Michellejoy Hughes for her
contribution to this edition.

The publishers would like to thank the following for permissions
to use copyright material:

Page make-up: GreenGate Publishing Services, Tonbridge, Kent
Illustrations: GreenGate Publishing Services, Tonbridge, Kent
Cover illustrations: Lo Cole

Although we have made every effort to trace and contact all
copyright holders before publication this has not been possible in all
cases. If notified, the publisher will rectify any errors or omissions at
the earliest opportunity.

Links to third party websites are provided by Oxford in good faith
and for information only. Oxford disclaims any responsibility for
the materials contained in any third party website referenced in
this work.

Introduction

What is Bond?

The Bond *Challenge* titles are the most stretching of the Bond assessment papers. Bond *Challenge* is carefully designed to stretch above and beyond the level provided in the regular Bond assessment range.

How does this book work?

The book contains two distinct sets of papers, along with fully explained answers and a Progress Chart:

- Focus tests, accompanied by advice and directions, which are focused on particular (and age-appropriate) Maths question types encountered in the 11[+] and other exams, but devised at a higher level than the standard Assessment papers. Each focus test is designed to help raise a child's skills in the question type as well as offer plenty of practice for the necessary techniques.

- Mixed papers, which are full-length tests containing a full range of Maths question types. These are designed to provide rigorous practice for children working at a level higher than that required to pass at the 11[+] and other Maths tests.

- Fully explained answers are provided for both types of test in the middle of the book.

- At the back of the book, there is a Progress Chart which allows you to track your child's progress.

- Some questions may require a ruler or a protractor. Calculators are not permitted.

How much time should the tests take?

The tests are for practice and to reinforce learning, and you may wish to test exam techniques and working to a set time limit. We would recommend your child spends 50 minutes to answer the 50 questions in each Mixed paper. You can reduce the suggested time by five minutes to practise working at speed.

Using the Progress Chart

The Progress Chart can be used to track Focus test and Mixed paper results over time to monitor how well your child is doing and identify any repeated problems in tackling the different question types.

When you compare, order and round whole numbers and decimals, look carefully at the value of each digit.

1 Write the heights of these mountains in order, starting with the highest.

Mountain	Height (feet)
Jannu	25 299
Kamet	25 446
Lhotse	27 940
Makalu	27 838
Nuptse	25 801

Mountain	Height (feet)

Use these four digits and the decimal point to answer both these questions.

There is one digit in front of the decimal point in each answer.

7   3   4   8   .

2 What is the largest possible decimal number you can make?

___ • ___ ___ ___

3 What is the decimal number that is as near as possible to 4?

___ • ___ ___ ___

Round each of these measurements to the nearest tenth.

4 12.75 cm _____   **5** 34.63 m _____   **6** 5.908 kg _____

Write the missing numbers in these calculations. Choose from 10, 100 or 1000.

7 46.93 ÷ _____ = 4.693   **8** 807.9 × _____ = 807 900

9 375.4 ÷ _____ = 3.754   **10** 3.09 × _____ = 3090

11 What is the value of the digit 5 in the number 23.05**6**? _____

12 I'm thinking of a number less than 1. The two digits total 9 and it rounds to 0.6 to the nearest tenth. What number is it? 0. ___ ___

Multiplication and division

If numbers are too large to multiply or divide mentally, use a written method and always estimate an approximate answer first.

1 Complete this multiplication grid.

×	7	12	30
9			
		96	
11	77		

2

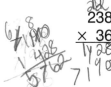

```
  238
× 36
```

Example:

```
   167
×   53
   501    (167 × 3)
  8350    (167 × 50)
  8851
```

3 What is 435 × 74?

×	400	30	5
70			
4			

Total: _____

Example: What is 236 × 23?

×	200	30	6	
20	4000	600	120	4720
3	600	90	18	708

Total: 5428

4 Circle the division that has a remainder of 2.

239 ÷ 27   548 ÷ 14   614 ÷ 19   307 ÷ 28

5 Write the missing digits.

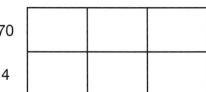

```
     4__ __.3__ __
16) 7 8 9 4
```

5

6 This length of ribbon is divided into four equal lengths. How long is each length? _____

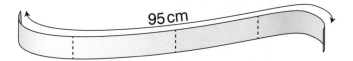

95 cm

7 What is the area of a square with sides of 12.5 cm?

12.5 cm

Area = _____

8 £573 is divided equally between four people.

How much do they each get? _____

9 Three identical books have a total weight of 2400 g.

What is the weight of five of these books? _____

10 A farmer collects 134 eggs and puts them into egg boxes. Each egg box holds 6 eggs.

How many egg boxes will he fill? _____

11 Alex saved £9.50 a week for 25 weeks.

How much has he saved altogether? _____

12 A lorry holds 1589 kg of sugar. It is divided equally into five containers.

How much sugar is in each container? _____

Factors, multiples and prime numbers

A prime number has only two factors, 1 and itself. The number 1 is not a prime number as it only has one factor.

1 Write the missing factors for 72.

(1, __) (__, __) (__, __) (__, __) (__, __) (__, __)

2 Write the numbers 3, 4, 6 and 9 to complete these.

184 is a multiple of _____.

243 is a multiple of _____ and _____.

276 is a multiple of _____, _____ and _____.

3 Write these numbers on the Venn diagram.

20   35   8   45   30   21   4

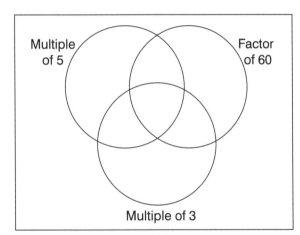

4 Here are all the pairs of factors for a number. Write the number and complete the missing factors.

_____ → (1, __) (2, __) (3, __) (4, 12) (6, __)

5 The lowest common multiple of 6 and 8 is 24.

What is the lowest common multiple of these pairs of numbers?

9 and 8 _____   5 and 4 _____   4 and 6 _____

The numbers 1, 2, 3 and 6 are common factors of 24 and 18.

The highest common factor (HCF) of 24 and 18 is 6.

List the common factors and circle the HCF for each of these sets of numbers.

6 Common factors of 72 and 48: _____

7 Common factors of 45, 36 and 90: _____

8 Which two factors of 144 have a total of 30? _____ and _____

Choose any of these prime numbers to complete the multiplications:

$$3 \quad 5 \quad 11 \quad 17 \quad 19$$

9 _____ × _____ × _____ = 1045

10 _____ × _____ × _____ = 561

11 Which three consecutive prime numbers multiply to make 385?

_____ × _____ × _____ = 385

12 What are the factors of the square numbers 4, 9 and 16?

4 _____

9 _____

16 _____

> **What do you notice about the factors of any square number?**

Fractions, decimals, percentages, ratios and proportions

To compare fractions with different denominators, change them to equivalent fractions with a common denominator.

Look at these number cards.

3   5   2   9

Use two of the cards to complete these.   **1** $\dfrac{\Box}{\Box} < \dfrac{1}{2}$ **2** $\dfrac{\Box}{\Box} = 0.6$

3 These are Sam's maths test scores as marks out of a total.

Convert each of the scores to a percentage.

37 out of 50 = _____   18 out of 20 = _____   21 out of 25 = _____

4 What is the ratio of grey tiles

to white tiles? _____

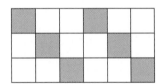

5 How many white tiles are needed if 90 tiles are used in this pattern?

_____

6 Write the missing digits to complete these.

$\dfrac{1}{\Box} = 0.\Box = 20\%$ $\dfrac{\Box}{4} = 0.75 = \Box\%$ $\dfrac{1}{20} = 0.\Box = \Box\%$

7 Answer these.

$\dfrac{3}{5} + \dfrac{2}{3} = \dfrac{\Box}{\Box}$ $\dfrac{3}{4} - \dfrac{1}{5} = \dfrac{\Box}{\Box}$ $\dfrac{1}{4} \times \dfrac{4}{5} = \dfrac{\Box}{\Box}$

8 This boat is drawn at a scale of 150:1. The drawing is 4cm long.

How long is the actual boat? _____

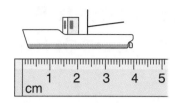

9 Sophie mixes 3 litres of white paint with every 5 litres of blue paint.

She needs 24 litres of paint altogether.

How many litres of blue paint will she need? _____

In this recipe each ingredient is given as a proportion of the total weight.

500g carrot cake

$\frac{1}{5}$ butter   100g

$\frac{1}{4}$ flour   _____ g

$\frac{1}{10}$ grated carrots   _____ g

$\frac{1}{20}$ sugar   _____ g

$\frac{2}{5}$ other ingredients   200g

10 Write the weight of each ingredient in the recipe.

11 Using this recipe, how many grams of butter would be needed for an 800g cake? _____

12 What fraction of £2 is each of these amounts?

10p _____   40p _____   £1.50 _____

Now go to the Progress Chart to record your score!   Total   12

A sequence is a list of numbers in a pattern. To find missing numbers look at the difference between the numbers.

1 What is the next number in this sequence?

37   22   7   −8   −23   _____

Write the missing numbers in these sequences.

2 248   _____   _____   98   48   −2   _____

3 _____   −2.8   −1.9   _____   −0.1   _____   1.7

4 _____   9   16   25   36   _____   _____

What is the difference in temperature between each pair of thermometers?

5 _____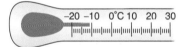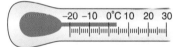

6 _____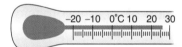

7 Which two square numbers total 100? _____ and _____

8 In this sequence you add the same amount each time.
Write the missing numbers.

5   _____   _____   _____   21

9 Will the number 41 be in this sequence? Circle the answer: yes   no

−9   −4   1   6   11   …

10 Each number is double the previous number. Write the missing numbers.

7   14   28   _____   _____   _____

11 What is 6^3? _____

12 What is the square root of 196? _____

Focus test 6 Equations and algebra

Josh made this shape pattern with counters.

The table shows the number of counters he used for each shape.

Shape number	1	2	3	4	n
Counters	1	3	5	7	?

1 What is the correct formula for this dot pattern? Circle the answer.

$3n - 3$ $n + 1$ $4n - 5$ $2n - 1$ $n + 2$

2 How many counters would there be for the 20th shape pattern? _____

Collect like terms to simplify these expressions.

3 $4c + 5 + 2a - c + 6$ _____

4 $3(5+y) + 4(y-3)$ _____

5 $b^2 - 4b - 3b + 4b^2$ _____

Find the value of these expressions if a = 3, b = 5, c = 1

6 abc _____

7 $2(ab) + 4c$ _____

8 $(3b - c) + a^2$ _____

9 $(4a - 2b)^2 + ab$ _____

Solve these equations.

10 $2n - 8 = 30$ $n =$ _____

11 $14 - 2y = 4$ $y =$ _____

12 Is this statement 'true' or 'false'? Circle the answer.

If *l* is the length of a rectangle and *w* is the width of the rectangle, the formula 2(*l* + *w*) gives the perimeter of the rectangle.

true   false

Focus test 7 Shapes and angles

Look for the properties of 2-D shapes, including length of sides, any parallel lines, angle sizes and lines of symmetry.

1 Write the letter for each of these shapes in the correct part of the Carroll diagram.

	Pentagon	Not a pentagon
1 or more lines of symmetry		
No lines of symmetry		

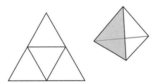

This is the net of a tetrahedron.

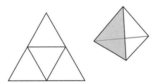

Write the name of each of these shapes from its net.

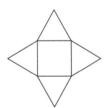

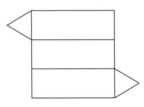

2 _____

3 _____

Two angles of this quadrilateral are 95° and 72°.

Measure the other two angles accurately using a protractor.

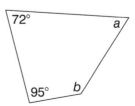

4 $a =$ _____

5 $b =$ _____

6 Here is part of a shape. Draw three more straight lines to make a shape with two lines of symmetry. Use a ruler.

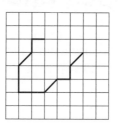

Rectangle ABCD has a diagonal line BC.
Calculate the size of angles x and y.

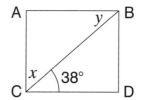

7 angle x = _____

8 angle y = _____

9 Is this statement 'always true', 'sometimes true' or 'never true'? Circle the answer.

An isosceles triangle has an obtuse angle.

always true   sometimes true   never true

AB and CD are parallel lines.

10 Which line is perpendicular to AB? _____

11 What is the angle z? _____

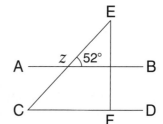

12 Look at this equilateral triangle inside a rectangle.

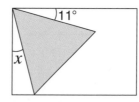

Calculate the value of x without using a protractor. _____

Area, perimeter and volume

Remember: Perimeter is measured in units such as centimetres (cm) and metres (m). Area is measured in square units such as cm^2 and m^2. Volume is measured in cubic units such as cm^3 and m^3.

Calculate the area and perimeter of this room.

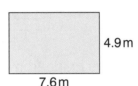

4.9 m

7.6 m

1 Area = _____

2 Perimeter = _____

3 What is the area of this triangle?

Area of triangle = _____

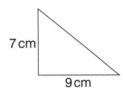

7 cm

9 cm

4 This star is made from a square and four triangles. What is the total area of the star?

_____

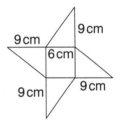

9 cm

9 cm

6 cm

9 cm

9 cm

5 What is the area of this garden, not including the pond?

_____

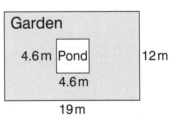

Garden

4.6 m | Pond

4.6 m

12 m

19 m

6 What is the area of this shape?

_____

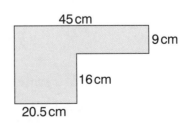

45 cm

9 cm

16 cm

20.5 cm

Note that none of the diagrams in this book are drawn to scale.

7 A cuboid has a square base with sides of 12 cm. The volume of the cuboid is 1152 cm³.

What is the height of the cuboid? _____

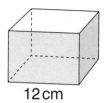

12 cm

8 On the grid draw a triangle with the same area as the rectangle. Use a ruler.

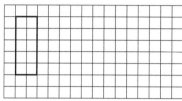

9 This shape is made from equilateral triangles and a square. The square has sides of 21 cm.

What is the perimeter of the shape?

_____

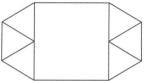

10 A square has sides of 105 mm.

What is the area of the square in square centimetres? _____

What is the perimeter of the square in centimetres? _____

11 A square has an area of 841 cm².

What is the length of each side? _____

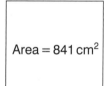

Area = 841 cm²

12 Calculate the difference in area of these two rooms.

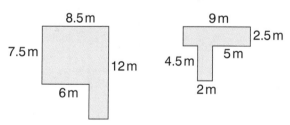

Area = _____   Area = _____

Difference = _____

Focus test 9   Measures

We still sometimes use imperial units such as pints, feet and pounds. These are measures that were used in the past. Try to learn their approximate metric values.

Write the amount shown on each scale.

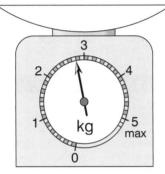

1 _____

2 _____

Give your answer in millilitres.

3 _____

4 _____

Complete these conversions.

5 675 mm = _____ cm

6 0.95 litres = _____ ml

7 84.8 m = _____ cm

8 3825 g = _____ kg

9 What is the length of this line in millimetres? _____

10 An athlete runs 15 laps of a 400 metre track. She wants to run a total of 10km.

How many more laps does she need to run? _____

Circle the closest approximation for these imperial to metric conversions.

11 A tree is 20 feet tall. Approximately how many metres is this?

  0.6m   60m   6m   3m   10m

12 Approximately how many miles are there in 160km?

  20 miles   100 miles   150 miles   300 miles   80 miles

Now go to the Progress Chart to record your score!   Total   12

Transformations and coordinates

Coordinates are useful for showing an exact position of a point on a grid or for plotting the vertices of shapes. Remember to read the numbers on the horizontal x-axis first, then the vertical y-axis.

Do these shapes show a translation, rotation or reflection? Circle each answer.

1

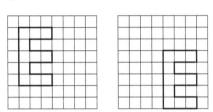

translation   rotation   reflection

2

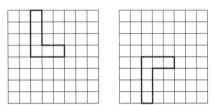

translation   rotation   reflection

3

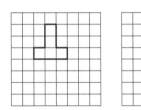

translation   rotation   reflection

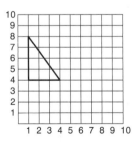

4 On the grid, draw another triangle at the coordinates: (9, 2), (6, 2) and (6, 6).

5 Is this triangle a translation, rotation or reflection of the first triangle?

_____

Here are two sides of a square.

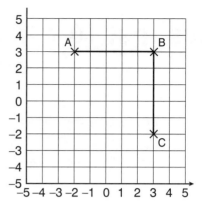

6 What are the coordinates of the three vertices?

A (__, __)   B (__, __)   C (__, __)

7 Mark the missing coordinates for the fourth vertex and complete the square.

8 What are the coordinates of the fourth vertex of the square?   D (__, __)

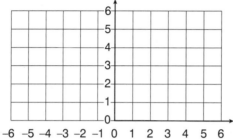

9 Plot these points on the grid and join them in order with a pencil and ruler.

(4, 1), (6, 4), (2, 4), (0, 1)

10 Reflect your drawing into the second quadrant and plot the points.

What are the coordinates of your shape?

(__, __)   (__, __)   (__, __)   (__, __)

11 Colour squares on this grid to reflect this shape in the mirror line.

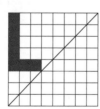

12 This is an isosceles triangle. Write in the missing coordinates.

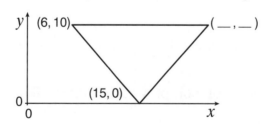

Take a moment to read each graph to make sure that you understand it before answering the questions.

This pie chart shows the number of goals scored by the top 5 players at a hockey tournament. These 5 players scored a total of **90 goals** between them.

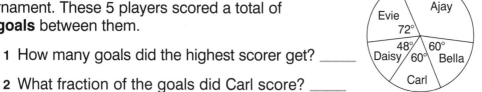

Goals scored by top 5 scorers

1 How many goals did the highest scorer get? _____

2 What fraction of the goals did Carl score? _____

3 What percentage of the goals did Evie score? _____

This frequency chart shows the number of goals scored by all the players in the hockey tournament.

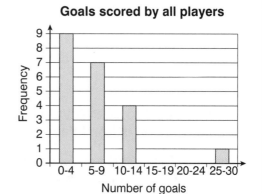

Goals scored by all players

4 How many players scored 5 or more goals but fewer than 10 goals?
_____

5 How many players altogether scored fewer than 10 goals? _____

6 Is this statement 'true', 'false' or is it 'impossible to say'? Circle the answer.

Three players did not score a goal.

     true   false   impossible to say

This graph shows the number of goals scored each minute in all 6 games of hockey in the tournament.

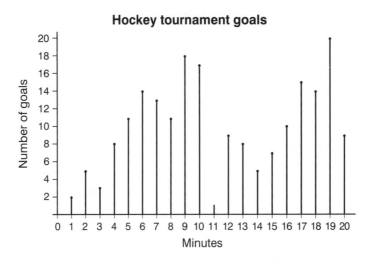

Hockey tournament goals

7 How many goals were scored in the first 5 minutes? _____

8 In which 3 minutes were the most goals scored? Circle the answer.

    8th–10th minutes   17th–19th minutes

9 In one particular minute the same number of goals was scored in all 6 games. How many goals were scored in each game in that one minute? _____

Look at **all** the graphs and charts and answer these questions. You need to decide which information is helpful for each task.

10 The goals of Evie, Carl and Bella are missing from the frequency chart. Look at the pie chart and use this information to complete the frequency chart.

11 There were 4 teams in the tournament. Use the completed frequency chart to work out how many players there were in each team. _____

12 Is this statement 'true', 'false' or is it 'impossible to say'? Circle the answer.

    Daisy scored one-third of her goals in the first minute.

        true   false   impossible to say

Focus test 12 — Mean, median, mode, range and probability

Number and price of ice creams sold

Flavour	vanilla	chocolate	cherry	lime	mint	peach	lemon
Number sold on Saturday	24	34	23	24	19	23	23
Number sold on Sunday	28	32	27	25	18	23	29
Price	£1.20	£1.55	£1.25	£1.40	£1.30	£1.35	£1.40

1 What is the mode of the number of ice creams sold on Saturday? _____

2 What is the mean number of ice creams sold on Sunday? _____

3 What is the median price of an ice cream? _____

4 Which day has the greatest range in the number of ice creams sold?

_____

This information is about the number of ice creams of each flavour sold on Monday.

Range: 12

Lowest number sold of one flavour: 15

Mode: 20

Mean: 19

Flavour	vanilla	chocolate	cherry	lime	mint	peach	lemon
Number sold on Monday	27	20			15	20	18

5–6 Work out the two missing numbers for the ice creams sold on Monday.
_____ and _____

> Remember: on a probability scale 0 is impossible, 1 is certain and the middle is 50/50 or an even chance.

This spinner has the numbers 1 to 6.

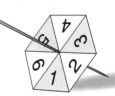

7 Draw an arrow on this probability scale to show the chance of spinning an odd number.

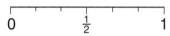

0      $\frac{1}{2}$ 1

8 Draw an arrow on this probability scale to show the chance of spinning the number 3.

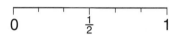

0      $\frac{1}{2}$ 1

9 What is the chance of spinning a 7 on the spinner? Circle the answer.

0      $\frac{1}{2}$ 1

These digit cards 1–9 are shuffled and placed face down.

10 What is the probability of picking an odd number from these digit cards? Circle the answer.

$$\frac{1}{2} \qquad \frac{4}{9} \qquad \frac{5}{9} \qquad \frac{2}{3}$$

11 What is the probability (expressed in lowest term fraction) of picking a multiple of 3 from these digit cards? _____

12 Which of these is **more likely**? Circle the answer.

spinning a 2 on the spinner

picking a 2 from the set of digit cards

Mixed paper 1

1–3 Write 14506 to the nearest 10, 100 and 1000.

14506	rounded to the nearest 10	_____
14506	rounded to the nearest 100	_____
14506	rounded to the nearest 1000	_____

4 I divide a number by 100. My answer is 84.7.

What is the number? _____

5 Write < or > to make this statement true.

1.101 __ 1.011

6   40.9
            × 2.8

7   1.96
            × 0.64

_____   _____

8 A mobile phone contract costs £13.50 each month. What is the total cost over a year? _____

9 (27 × 15) − 5 = _____

10 (33 × 26) + 2 = _____

11 What is the highest common factor of 16 and 48? _____

12 What are the factors of 128? _____

13 What is the lowest common multiple of 50 and 60? _____

14 Which 3 prime numbers under 25 can be multiplied together to make 897? _____ _____ _____

15 Write the next prime number after 47. _____

16 $\dfrac{6}{7} + \dfrac{5}{6} - \dfrac{1}{3} =$ _____

17–18 At the end of the year, Year 5 and Year 6 have earned house points in the ratio 2:3. There were a total of 750 house points awarded. How many did Year 5 and Year 6 each earn? Year 5 = _____ Year 6 = _____

Write the missing digits to complete these.

19 $\dfrac{3}{\boxed{}} = 0.3 = \boxed{}\%$

20 $\dfrac{1}{\boxed{}} = 0.\boxed{} = 25\%$

Complete these sequences.

21–22 32 64 128 256 512 _____ _____

23–24 1 2 4 7 11 16 _____ _____

25 What is 8^3? _____

What number does each letter represent?

26 $6r + 4r = 70$ $r =$ ___

27 $8s - 3s = 90$ $s =$ ___

28 $36t \div 4 = 54$ $t =$ ___

29 What is the **area** of this rectangle? _____

30 What is the **perimeter** of this rectangle? _____

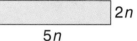
$2n$
$5n$

Look at this regular polygon.

31 What is the name of this whole shape? _____

32 How many lines of symmetry are there on this whole shape? _____

33 What is the name of the quadrilateral made from 3 triangles?

_____

34 What is the name of the quadrilateral made from 2 triangles?

_____

35 Calculate the size of angle x without using a protractor. _____

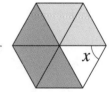

Calculate the area of these triangles.

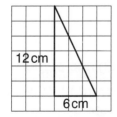

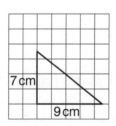

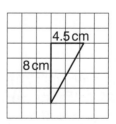

36 _____   **37** _____   **38** _____

A garden is a rectangular plot 7.8m long and 2.5m wide.

39 What is the area of the garden? ____________

40 Fencing is sold in 1m lengths. How many 1m lengths of fencing would be needed to go all the way round the garden? ____________

2

Fill in each space with one of these signs. < > =

41 0.8m ___ 75cm **42** 2901g ___ 2.91kg

2

Look at these weights.

12000g 2.01kg 12kg 2100g 20.1kg

43 Which weight is the heaviest? ____________

44 Which two weights are the same? ____________ and ____________

2

45 A man is 6 feet tall. Circle the closest approximation in metric units.

2000cm 20m 2m 200m 0.2m

1

A café sold 200 sandwiches. This pie chart shows the number of each type of filling.

Sandwich sales

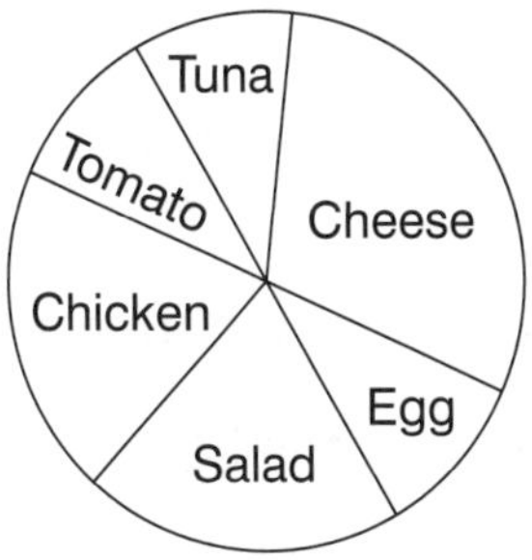

46 What percentage of sandwiches were filled with cheese? ____

47 How many chicken sandwiches were sold? ____

48 What fraction of the sandwiches were salad? Express the fraction in its lowest terms. $\frac{\square}{\square}$

49 How many more cheese and tuna sandwiches were sold than tomato and chicken? ____

50 An extra 40 egg sandwiches were sold. Now, what percentage of the sandwiches were egg? ____

5

Now go to the Progress Chart to record your score! Total 50

Mixed paper 2

1 I am thinking of a number that has all three digits in consecutive order. It rounds to 3.5 to the nearest tenth.

What is the number? ___ . ___ ___

1

2 Circle the smallest number.

$$38.05 \qquad 3.8 \qquad 35.08 \qquad 3.05 \qquad 5.83 \qquad 3.085$$

1

Write 10, 100 or 1000 to complete these calculations.

3 $230.7 \div$ _____ $= 2.307$

4 $59.041 \times$ _____ $= 590.41$

5 $996.2 \div$ _____ $= 0.9962$

3

6–8 Complete the pyramid. Each pair of numbers on the bottom row is multiplied together to form the number on the row above.

	0.048	
0.06		_____
0.3	_____	_____

3

9 There are 12 packs of paper in a box and 575 sheets of paper in each pack.

How many sheets of paper are there in a box? _____

10 A driver travels a total of 29.5 km each day.

How far does he travel in five days? _____

2

11–12 Write the numbers 7, 8 or 9 to make this statement true: 288 is a multiple of ___ and ___.

2

Year 5 are counting in 5s. Year 6 are counting in 6s and Year 7 are counting in 7s.

13 What is the lowest common multiple that Year 5 and Year 6 share? _____

14 What is the lowest common multiple that Year 6 and Year 7 share? _____

15 What is the lowest common multiple that Year 5, Year 6 and Year 7 share? _____

3

What fraction of 2m is each of these lengths?

16 20cm _____   **17** 50cm _____   **18** 40cm _____   ◯ 3

Orange drink is made using orange cordial and sparkling water in a mixture of one part orange cordial to five parts sparkling water. Fruit Bowl is made using orange drink and fresh pineapple juice in a mixture of two parts orange drink to three parts fresh pineapple juice.

19 If Ameera has a 1 litre bottle of orange cordial, how much orange drink can she make? _____

20 How much Fruit Bowl can she make? _____   ◯ 2

21 Circle the cube number in this set of numbers.

           46   48   24   64   86   44   ◯ 1

Write the missing numbers in these sequences.

22–23 ___   −21   −9   ___   15   27

24–25 8   ___   −4   −10   ___   −22   ◯ 4

    26 What is the difference between −13 and 5? ___   ◯ 1

The T-shapes in this sequence are made with interlocking cubes.

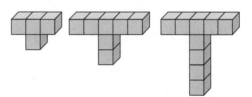

This table shows the number of cubes used for each shape.

Shape number	1	2	3	4	n
Cubes	4	7	10	___	?

27 How many cubes are needed for the 4th shape in this sequence? Write your answer in the table.

28 What is the correct formula for this T-shape sequence? Circle the answer.

       $n + 3$ $4n − 1$ $3n + 1$ $n + 4$ $2n − 3$

29 How many cubes will there be in the 10th shape? ___   ◯ 3

30–31 Underline the two equations that give the same answer.

      $(a + b) × c$ $ab + c$ $a (b + c)$ $(a × b) + c$ $a + (b × c)$ ◯ 2

Name each angle. Choose from **acute**, **obtuse**, **reflex**, or **right angle.**

32  _____

33  _____

34  _____

35  _____

4

36 Write **always**, **sometimes** or **never** to make this sentence true.

An isosceles triangles _____ has a right-angle.

1

Measure each line to the nearest 5 mm. Use a ruler.

37 ———————————————————————————— _____ mm

38 ———————————————————— _____ mm

39 What is the difference in length between these two lines? Write your answer in centimetres. _____

3

40 Circle the largest amount.

370 ml   3.07 litres   7300 ml   37 000 ml   7.3 litres

1

41 Circle the longer distance.   50 kilometres   50 miles

1

42–44 Translate this shape 2 squares down and 4 squares to the right.

Write the coordinates of the vertices of your translated shape.

(__, __) (__, __) (__, __)

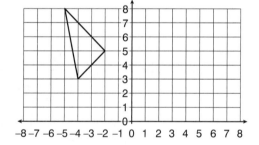

3

45 Is shape B a translation, rotation or reflection of shape A?

_____

46 Another shape has vertices at the coordinates (−2, −4) (0, −4) (0, −5) (2, −5) (2, −7) (−2, −7).

Is this shape a translation, rotation or reflection of shape A?

_____

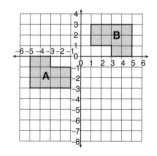

2

This graph shows the typical monthly temperatures in the UK.

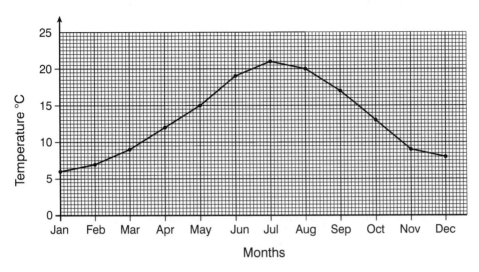

Months

47 What is the mean temperature for the whole year? _____

48 What is the median temperature for the whole year? _____

49 What temperature is the mode? _____

50 What is the temperature range over the whole year? _____ 4

Now go to the Progress Chart to record your score! Total 50

Mixed paper 3

Complete these sequences.

1 0.02   0.22   0.42   0.62   0.82   _____

2 0.25   0.375   0.5   0.625   0.75   _____

3 0.001   0.01   0.1   _____

4 What is the value of **7** in 36.704? _____

5 There are 20 232 books in a library, shelved in equal numbers on 24 bookcases. How many books are in each bookcase? _____

6 Four parcels each weigh 1.45 kg. What is the total weight of the four parcels? _____

7 A football tournament has 18 teams. Each team has 11 players and 2 substitutes. How many footballers in total will there be in the tournament? _____

8 A school buys 34 new computers costing £189 each. What is the total cost for these computers? _____

9 Jyoti multiplied a number by 8 instead of dividing a number by 8. Her answer was 3648. What should her answer have been? _____

10–12 Circle the numbers that are factors of 28.

2   3   4   5   6   7   8   9

13 What number has these factors, 1 and itself? _____

2, 3, 4, 6, 9, 12, 18

14–15 Circle the numbers that are **not** prime numbers.

7   27   37   47   57

Change these fractions into decimals.

16 $\dfrac{34}{20}$ = _____

17 $\dfrac{9}{36}$ = _____

Change these survey results into percentages.

18 37 out of 50 children preferred strawberry jam to raspberry jam. _____ %

19 18 out of 25 bus passengers bought return tickets. _____ %

20 8 out of 20 pet owners had a cat and a dog. _____ %

Any answer that requires units of measurement should be marked wrong if the correct units have not been included.

Focus Test 1: Place value (page 4)

1.

Mountain	Height (feet)
Lhotse	27 940
Makalu	27 838
Nuptse	25 801
Kamet	25 446
Jannu	25 229

To order numbers from smallest to largest, place them on a decimal grid. Begin with the smallest numbers on the far left and work towards the right.

TTh	Th	H	T	U
2	5	2	9	9
2	5	4	4	6
2	7	9	4	0
2	7	8	3	8
2	5	8	0	1

2. **8.743** Begin with the largest number on the left and work towards the right, using the next-largest number each time.

3. **3.874** 3.8 is closer to 4.0 than 4.3, so begin with the 3 in the ones column and fill in the other numbers, with the largest first.

4–6 When rounding a number to the nearest tenth, look at the number in the hundredths column. If it is 4 or below, leave the number in the tenths column unchanged. If it is 5 or above, raise the number in the tenths column by 1.

4. **12.8 cm**

5. **34.6 m**

6. **5.9 kg**

7. **10** To divide a number by 10, move all of the numbers on the decimal grid 1 place to the right.

8. **1000** To multiply a number by 1000, move all of the numbers on the decimal grid 3 places to the left.

9. **100** To divide a number by 100, move all of the numbers on the decimal grid 2 places to the right.

10. **1000** See Q8.

11. $\frac{5}{100}$ *or* **5 hundredths** Place the number on a decimal grid to locate the 5.

T	U	•	t	h	th
2	3	•	0	5	6

12. **0.63** Find the pairs of digits that add up to 9 (0 + 9, 1 + 8, 2 + 7, 3 + 6, 4 + 5) and use them to make 2-digit numbers (09, 90, 18, 81, 27, 72, 36, 63, 45, 54). To round to 0.6 to the nearest tenth, the first digit must be either a 6 with a number less than 5 in the hundredths column to round down, or a 5 with a number more than 4 in the hundredths column to round up. The digits must be 63.

Focus Test 2: Multiplication and division (pages 5–6)

1.

×	7	12	30
9	63	108	270
8	56	96	240
11	77	132	330

Divide 96 by 12 to find 8 in the far left column. Next, complete the grid by multiplying each number in the top row by the number in the far left column.

2. **8568**

```
      2  3  8
   ×     3  6
   1  4  2  8
   7  1  4  0
   8  5  6  8
```

3. **32 190**

×	400	30	5	
70	28 000	2100	350	30 450
4	1600	120	20	1740
				32 190

4. **548 ÷ 14** Work logically by taking 2 from each large number, for the remainder, then dividing each number until there is a number that divides exactly.

5.

```
            4  9  3  .  3  7  5
   16 | 7  8  9  4
        6  4
        1  4  9
        1  4  4
           5  4
           4  8
           0  6  0
              4  8
              1  2  0
              1  1  2
                 8  0
                 8  0
                    0
```

EXPANDED ANSWERS

Bond Maths Assessment Papers Challenge 10–11+ years

6 **23.75 cm** Divide 95 cm by 4.

```
      2   3  .  7   5
   ┌─────────────────
 4 │  9   5  .  0   0
           1     3   2
```

7 **156.25 cm²** To find the area, multiply the
length by the width. In a square, the length
and width are the same. To multiply by a
decimal number, work the multiplication
without the decimal point. At the end, count
the number of digits after the decimal point in
the question and make sure the answer has
the same number of digits after the decimal
point. Here there are two digits after the
decimal point in the question, so there must
be two digits after the decimal point in the
answer (15625 becomes 156.25).

```
            1   2   5
        ×   1   2   5
        ─────────────
            6   2   5
        2   5   0   0
    1   2   5   0   0
    ─────────────────
    1   5   6   2   5
```

8 **£143.25** Divide £573 by 4.
9 **4000 g** or **4 kg** Divide the 2400 g by 3 to find
the weight of 1 book, then multiply this by 5 to
find the weight of 5 books (2400 g ÷ 3 = 800 g;
800 g × 5 = 4000 g or 4 kg).
10 **22** Divide 134 by 6, but only include whole
numbers of boxes and no remainders
(134 ÷ 6 = 22 r 2, which is 22 full boxes).
11 **£237.50** Multiply £9.50 by 25. See Q7.
12 **317.8 kg** Divide 1589 kg by 5.

Focus Test 3 : Factors, multiples and prime numbers (pages 7–8)

1 **(1, 72) (2, 36) (3, 24) (4, 18) (6, 12) (8, 9)** Factors
are the pairs of numbers that fit exactly into
another number without a remainder.
2 **4; 3 and 9; 3, 4 and 6** Multiples are numbers
that appear in a particular number's times table.
They are how many times a number is multiplied.

3
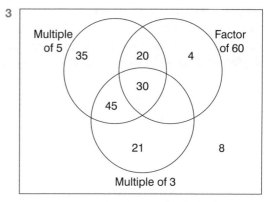

20 is a multiple of 5 and a factor of 60, so it
goes where these two circles overlap, but not
in the section that also overlaps the circle for
multiples of 3. **35** is a multiple of 5 only, so it
goes in the far left space of the circle. **8** is not
a multiple of 5 or 3 and is not a factor of 60,
so it goes outside of the circles. **45** is both a
multiple of 5 and a multiple of 3, so it goes
where these two circles overlap, but not in the
section that also overlaps the circle for factors
of 60. **30** is a multiple of 3 and 5 and a factor
of 60, so it goes in the central section where
all three circles overlap. **21** is a multiple of 3
only, so it goes in the lowest part of the circle.
4 is a factor of 60 only, so it goes in the far
right of the circle.
4 **48 (1, 48) (2, 24) (3, 16) (4, 12) (6, 8)** The key
is 4 and 12 because this shows the number
to be 48, and then the other factors can be
found.
5 **72, 20, 12** To find the lowest common multiple
(LCM), list the multiples of two or more
numbers and locate the lowest number that is
shared by each number.
9: 9, 18, 27, 36, 45, 54, 63, **72**
8: 8, 16, 24, 32, 40, 48, 56, 64, **72**
5: 5, 10, 15, **20**
4: 4, 8, 12, 16, **20**
4: 4, 8, **12**
6: 6, **12**
6–7 To find the highest common factor (HCF) of
two or more numbers, list the factors that fit
into each number in order from smallest to
largest. Then highlight the factors that are
shared and locate the highest one.
6 **1, 2, 3, 4, 6, 8, 12, ㉔**
Factors of 72: **1, 2, 3, 4, 6, 8**, 9, **12**, 18, **24**,
36, 72
Factors of 48: **1, 2, 3, 4, 6, 8, 12**, 16, **24**, 48

7 **1, 3,⑨**
   Factors of 45: **1, 3**, 5, **9**, 15, 45
   Factors of 36: **1**, 2, **3**, 4, 6, **9**, 12, 18, 36
   Factors of 90: **1**, 2, **3**, 5, 6, **9**, 10, 15, 18, 30, 45, 90

8 **12 and 18** *or* **6 and 24** Find the factors of 144 (1, 2, 3, 6, 8, 9, 12, 16, 18, 24) and add them together until you have a pair that adds up to 30. (36, 48 and 72 are also factors of 144 but they are too large to add to something else making 30.)

9–10 **5 × 11 × 19, 3 × 11 × 17** Any number ending in 5 has 5 as a factor, and 5 is a prime number. Any number for which the digits added together gives a result that is in the 3 times table has 3 as a factor, and 3 is a prime number.

11 **5 × 7 × 11** The 5 can be identified as the number ends in 5. The digits do not add up to a multiple of 3, so 5 must be the first of the consecutive prime numbers.

12 **1, 2, 4; 1, 3, 9; 1, 2, 4, 8, 16**
   Square numbers always have an odd number of factors This is because a square number is multiplied by itself, so that is a single number and not a pair.

Focus Test 4 : Fractions, decimals, percentages, ratios and proportions (page 9–10)

1 $\frac{2}{5}$ **or** $\frac{2}{9}$ **or** $\frac{3}{9}$ Use any of the cards to make a fraction that is less than a half.

2 $\frac{3}{5}$ To convert a decimal to a fraction, place the decimal on a decimal grid and then create a fraction in tenths, hundredths or thousandths. Then reduce the fraction to its simplest form and find an equivalent fraction using the cards $\left(0.6 = \frac{6}{10} = \frac{3}{5}\right)$.

3 **74%, 90%, 84%** Use multiplication to convert each score to an equivalent mark out of 100. The numerator is then a percentage $\left(\frac{37}{50} = \frac{74}{100} = 74\%; \frac{18}{20} = \frac{90}{100} = 90\%; \frac{21}{25} = \frac{84}{100} = 84\%\right)$.

4 **1:2** To find the ratio, count the number of grey tiles and put this first, followed by a colon. Next, count the number of white tiles and put that after the colon. Finally, put the ratio in its simplest form (6:12 = 1:2).

5 **60** Add together the ratios to make a group, then divide this group into the total to find how many times it fits (1 + 2 = 3; 90 tiles ÷ 3 = 30). Finally, multiply this answer by the individual parts of the ratio (30 × 1 = 30 grey tiles; 30 × 2 = 60 white tiles).

6 $\frac{1}{5} = 0.2 = 20\%, \frac{3}{4} = 0.75 = 75\%, \frac{1}{20} = 0.05 = 5\%$ Begin with the known fraction, decimal or percentage and work out the missing information from that (20% = 0.2 = $\frac{1}{5}$; 75% = 0.75 = $\frac{3}{4}$; $\frac{1}{20} = \frac{5}{100} = 0.05 = 5\%$).

7 $1\frac{4}{15}, \frac{11}{20}, \frac{1}{5}$ To add or subtract fractions, first find equivalent fractions so that the bottom numbers (the denominators) are the same. Remember to only add or subtract the numerators, not the denominators, and to put the answer in its simplest form $\left(\frac{3}{5} = \frac{9}{15}\right.$ and $\frac{2}{3} = \frac{10}{15}; \frac{9}{15} + \frac{10}{15} = \frac{19}{15} = 1\frac{4}{15}; \frac{3}{4} = \frac{15}{20}$ and $\frac{1}{5} = \frac{4}{20}; \frac{15}{20} - \frac{4}{20} = \frac{11}{20}\left.\right)$. To multiply fractions, multiply the numerators and the denominators, then place the answer in its simplest form $\left(\frac{1}{4} \times \frac{4}{5} = \frac{4}{20} = \frac{1}{5}\right)$.

8 **600 cm** or **6 m** Multiply every 1 cm by 150 (4 cm × 150 = 600 cm or 6 m).

9 **15 litres** See Focus Test 4, Q5. 3 + 5 = 8; 24 ÷ 8 = 3; 3 × 3 = 9 litres of white paint; 3 × 5 = 15 litres of blue paint.

10 $\frac{1}{4}$ flour = **125 g**, $\frac{1}{10}$ grated carrots = **50 g**, $\frac{1}{20}$ sugar = **25 g** If $\frac{1}{5} = 100$ g and the whole cake weighs 500 g, everything else is proportional. $\frac{1}{4}$ of 500 g = 125 g, $\frac{1}{10}$ of 500 g = 50 g and $\frac{1}{20}$ of 500 g = 25 g.

11 **160 g** If the cake is an 800 g cake, the proportions are still the same, and $\frac{1}{5}$ of 800 is 160 g.

12 $\frac{1}{20}, \frac{1}{5}, \frac{3}{4}$ Create a fraction and then place it in its simplest form (£2 = 200p, so 10p = $\frac{10}{200} = \frac{1}{20}$; 40p = $\frac{40}{200} = \frac{1}{5}$; £1.50 = $\frac{150}{200} = \frac{3}{4}$).

Focus Test 5 : Special numbers and number sequences (page 11)

1–4 First work out the sequence between the given numbers. Then use the same rule to find the missing number.

1 **−38** From 37 to 22 = −15, from 22 to 7 = −15, etc., so −23 − 15 = −38.

2 **198, 148, −52** From 98 to 48 = −50 and from 48 to −2 = −50, so 248 − 50 = 198, 198 − 50 = 148 and −2 − 50 = −52.

3 **−3.7, −1, 0.8,** From −2.8 to −1.9 = +0.9, so −2.8 − 0.9 = −3.7, −1.9 + 0.9 = −1 and −1 + 0.9 = 0.8.

4 **4, 49, 64** This sequence is square numbers. $2^2 = 4$, $7^2 = 49$ and $8^2 = 64$.

5–6 Work out the negative numbers to 0, then add on the positive numbers from 0.

5 **15°C** From –11°C to 0°C = 11°C and from 0°C to 4°C = 4°C, so 11°C + 4°C = 15°C.

6 **40°C** From –14°C to 0°C = 14°C and from 0°C to 26°C = 26°C, so 14°C + 26°C = 40°C.

7 **36, 64** List the square numbers that are less than 100, then find any pairs of numbers that begin with digits that, when combined, are close to 100. Cross out any numbers that do not fit (~~1, 4, 9, 16, 25~~, 36, 49, 64, ~~81~~). Check the remaining pairs to see if they add up to 100.

8 **9, 13, 17** Subtract the first number from the last (21 – 5 = 16). Then, divide 16 by the 4 steps that lead from 5 to 21 (16 ÷ 4 = 4). Finally, add on 4 each time to find the missing numbers (5 + 4 = $\underline{9}$; 9 + 4 = $\underline{13}$; 13 + 4 = $\underline{17}$; 17 + 4 = $\underline{21}$).

9 **yes** As the sequence rule is "add 5 each time", the positive numbers will all end in 6 or 1, so 41 will fit in this sequence.

10 **56, 112, 224** 28 × 2 = $\underline{56}$; 56 × 2 = $\underline{112}$; 112 × 2 = $\underline{224}$

11 **216** A cube number is a number multiplied by itself, then multiplied by itself again (6 × 6 = 36; 36 × 6 = 216).

12 **14** A square number is a number multiplied by itself, and a square root is the number that has been multiplied by itself. As 12 × 12 = 144, the square root of 196 must be larger than 12. Multiply 13 × 13 = 169, which is closer, then try 14 × 14 = 196 to find the correct answer.

Focus Test 6: Equations and algebra (page 12)

1 **2n – 1**

Shape number	1	2	3	4	n
Counters	1	3	5	7	?

The top row is called *n*. It just means the number in the sequence (first, second, third, fourth, etc.)

The bottom row is called the sequence.

First, work out the difference of the sequence (1 to 3 = +2), which is to add 2 each time. This is the first part of the formula, so put this number in front of n to make 2n. Make $n = 1$ (the first term of the sequence). If n = 1, then 2n = 2 (2 × 1 = 2). Now look at the number of counters in the first sequence, which is 1. To get from 2 (2n = 2 × 1 = 2) to 1, subtract 1. This is the final part of the formula, so put – 1 after the 2n. The formula is 2n – 1.

2 **39** Make n = 20. If n = 20, then 2n – 1 = 39 (2 × 20 – 1 = 39).

3–5 To collect like terms, add or subtract all the individual letters and all the numbers. Square or cube numbers can only be added together with other square or cube numbers. Any number or letter outside of a bracket is multiplied with each number or letter inside the bracket first. It does not matter which order the final letters and numbers are placed in.

3 **2a + 3c + 11** 4c – c = 3c and 5 + 6 = 11, so it simplifies to 2a + 3c + 11.

4 **3 + 7y** 3 × 5 = 15; 3 × y = 3y; 4 × y = 4y; 4 × –3 = –12; then 15 + 3y + 4y – 12 simplifies to 3 + 7y.

5 **5b² – 7b** $b^2 + 4b^2 = 5b^2$ and –4b – 3b = –7b, so it simplifies to $5b^2 - 7b$.

6–9 When letters are together, they should be multiplied. Replace the letters with the numbers given, then complete the equation, remembering to work out brackets and square or cube numbers first.

6 **15** abc means 3 × 5 × 1 = 15.

7 **34** 2(ab) + 4c means 2 (3 × 5) + (4 × 1) = (2 × 15) + 4 = 30 + 4 = 34.

8 **23** $(3b – c) + a^2$ means $(3 \times 5 – 1) + 3^2 = (15 – 1) + 9 = 14 + 9 = 23$.

9 **19** $(4a – 2b)^2 + ab$ means $((4 \times 3) – (2 \times 5))^2 + (3 \times 5) = (12 – 10)^2 + 15 = 4 + 15 = 19$.

10–11 To solve substitution equations, there are three rules. First, keep letters on one side of the equal sign and numbers on the other. Second, to remove a negative number or letter, add the same number or letter and to remove a positive number or letter, subtract the same number or letter. Third, whatever action is done to one side of the equal sign, the same must be done to the other side.

10 **19** If 2n – 8 = 30, add 8 to both sides to get rid of –8. That gives 2n = 38, so divide 38 by 2 to find n (= 19).

11 **5** If 14 – 2y = 4, add 2y to both sides to get rid of –2y. That gives 14 = 4 + 2y, so subtract 4 from both sides to leave 10 = 2y. Now divide 10 by 2 to find y (= 5).

12 **true** The perimeter of a rectangle is found by adding up both lengths and both widths, so the formula 2(l + w) is correct as this is the same as 2 × length + 2 × width.

Focus Test 7: Shapes and angles (pages 13–14)

1

	Pentagon	Not a pentagon
1 or more lines of symmetry	B, E	A, D, F
No lines of symmetry	G	C

The equilateral triangle A is not a pentagon as it has 3 sides, not 5, but it has 3 lines of symmetry, so it fits in the top right box. The regular pentagon B has 5 lines of symmetry, so it fits into the top left box. The parallelogram C has 4 sides and no lines of symmetry. The regular hexagon D has 6 sides and 6 lines of symmetry. The pentagon E is not regular but it does have 1 line of symmetry. The kite F has 4 sides and 1 line of symmetry. The pentagon G is not regular and has no lines of symmetry.

2 **square-based pyramid** A square-based pyramid has a square base, four triangular faces and five vertices.

3 **triangular prism** A triangular prism has a triangular top, a base with three faces and six vertices.

4–5 **60°, 133°** Angle a is an acute angle and angle b is an obtuse angle, which helps as a check against protractor measurements. All 4-sided shapes have angles that add up to 360°, which provides a further check.

6

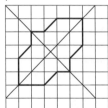

7 **52°** A rectangle has four right angles. Angle C is 90°, so angle x is 90° – 38° = 52°.

8 **38°** The three angles in a triangle add up to 180°. Angle y is 180° – 90° – 52° = 38°.

9 **sometimes true** An isosceles triangle has two angles the same and one different. It is sometimes true that one angle could be an obtuse angle, such as this example which has two angles of 25° and one angle of 130°.

10 **EF** A perpendicular line meets another line at a right angle.

11 **128°** Angles in a straight line add up to 180°. Angle z is 180° – 52° = 128°.

12 **19°** The right angle has an equilateral triangle inside and each angle of an equilateral triangle is 60°. Angle x must be 90° – 60° – 11° = 19°.

Focus Test 8: Area, perimeter and volume (pages 15–16)

1 **37.24 m²** Multiply the length by the width to find the area (7.6 m × 4.9 m = 37.24 m²).

2 **25.0 m** Add up the 2 lengths and the 2 widths to find the perimeter (7.6 m + 4.9 m + 7.6 m + 4.9 m = 25 m).

3 **31.5 cm²** The area of a triangle is length multiplied by width, then divided by 2 (9 cm × 7 cm = 63 cm²; 63 cm² ÷ 2 = 31.5 cm²).

4 **144 cm²** First work out the area of the square (6 cm × 6 cm = 36 cm²). Then work out the area of each triangle (9 cm × 6 cm ÷ 2 = 27 cm²). Finally, add together 4 stars and 1 square (36 cm² + 27 cm² + 27 cm² + 27 cm² + 27 cm² = 144 cm²).

5 **206.84 m²** First, work out the area of the garden (19 m × 12 m = 228 m²) and the area of the pond (4.6 m × 4.6 m = 21.16 m²). Then subtract the area of the pond from the area of the garden (228 m² – 21.16 m² = 206.84 m²).

6 **733 cm²** Divide the shape into two rectangles and use logic to place any measurements needed. Work out the area of each, then add them together (512.50 cm² + 220.50 cm² = 733 cm²). For example:

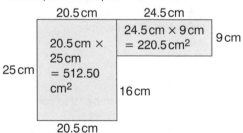

7 **8 cm** The volume of a cuboid is the length × width × height. This cuboid has a square base, so 12 cm × 12 cm = 144 cm². Divide the volume by the length and the width to find the height (1152 cm³ ÷ 144 cm² = 8 cm).

8 ***Any triangle that has an area of 10 cm*** The area of a triangle is height × base ÷ 2. So, the height of the triangle multiplied by the base must equal 20 (e.g. 2 × 10 or 4 × 5).

9 **105 cm** The top and bottom of the square are each 21 cm, and the sides of each triangle are 10.5 cm (21 cm ÷ 2). That makes the total perimeter (2 × 21 cm) + (6 × 10.5 cm) = 105 cm.

10 **110.25 cm², 42 cm** Convert the mm into centimetres by dividing by 10 (105 mm = 10.5 cm). Multiply the two sides to find the area (10.5 cm × 10.5 cm = 110.25 cm²). Then add up the four sides to find the perimeter (10.5 + 10.5 + 10.5 + 10.5 = 42 cm).

11 **29 cm** To find the square root of 841, begin with logical estimates. Multiples of 10 are easier to work out quickly. 10 × 10 = 100, which is too low. 20 × 20 = 400, which is too low. 30 × 30 = 900, which is only just over. Try going down by 1 (29 × 29 = 841) to find the correct answer.

12 **75 m², 31.5 m², 43.5 m²** See Focus Test 8, Q6.

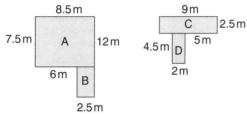

A = 8.5 m × 7.5 m = 63.75 m²
B = 2.5 m × 4.5 m = 11.25 m²
TOTAL = 75 m²

C = 9 m × 2.5 m = 22.5 m²
D = 4.5 m × 2 m = 9 m²
TOTAL = 31.5 m²

Focus Test 9: Measures (pages 17–18)

1–4 Look at the number of increments between the whole numbers on each scale and work out the value of each increment to add to the preceding whole number.

1 **2.8 kg**
2 **41.25 kg**
3 **1400 ml**
4 **2750 ml**
5 **67.5** Divide 675 mm by 10 to convert millimetres to centimetres.
6 **950** Multiply 0.95 litres by 1000 to convert litres to millilitres.
7 **8480** Multiply 84.8 metres by 100 to convert metres to centimetres.
8 **3.825** Divide 3825 g by 1000 to convert grams to kilograms.
9 **67 mm** The line is 6.7 cm, so multiply by 10 to convert centimetres to millimetres.
10 **10 laps** Multiply 15 by 400 metres to find the total length of laps already run (15 × 400 m = 6000 m). Next, convert 10 km into metres by multiplying by 1000 (10 km = 10 000 m). Subtract the laps already run from the total distance (10 000 m – 6000 m = 4000 m).

Finally, divide the answer by 400 metres to find the number of laps that she needs to run (4000 m ÷ 400 m = 10 laps).
11 **6 m** As a quick estimate, there are 3.3 feet to 1 m, so 20 feet is roughly 6 m.
12 **100 miles** As a quick estimate, there are 1.6 km in 1 mile, so 160 km is roughly 100 miles.

Focus Test 10: Transformations and coordinates (pages 19–20)

1 **translation** A translation moves a shape upwards, downwards or side to side, but it does not change its appearance. The E shape has moved down and to the right.
2 **reflection** A reflection mirrors a shape's image horizontally, vertically or diagonally. The L shape has been reflected in the y-axis.
3 **rotation** A rotation turns a shape in a circle around a fixed point (the centre of rotation). A rotation can rotate clockwise or anticlockwise, often by 90° (a quarter turn), 180° (a half turn) or 270° (a three-quarters turn). The T shape has been rotated 90° clockwise.
4 When plotting coordinates on a grid, use the rule "along the corridor and up the stairs" to remember to go horizontal, then vertical.

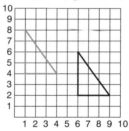

5 **translation** The triangle has moved down and to the right.
6 **A (–2, 3), B (3, 3), C (3, –2)**
7

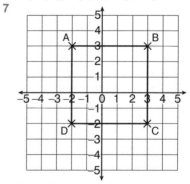

8 **(–2, –2)**

9
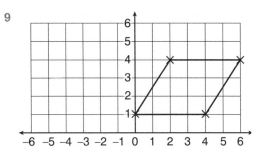

10 **(−4, 1), (−6, 4), (−2, 4), (0, 1)** When working with quadrants, begin in the top right-hand corner with quadrant 1. Moving anticlockwise, the top left-hand corner is quadrant 2. (If the question used more quadrants, the bottom left-hand corner would be quadrant 3 and the bottom right-hand corner would be quadrant 4.)

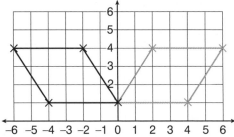

11

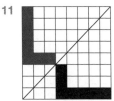

12 **(24, 10)** Find the distance between the x-axis of the far left coordinate and the bottom coordinate (6 to 15 is +9). As the triangle is an isosceles triangle, the distance from the centre coordinate to the one on the far right must be the same (15 + 9 = 24). The y-axis coordinate is the same as the first coordinate (10), so the missing coordinates are (24, 10).

Focus Test 11: Charts, graphs and tables (pages 21–22)

1 **30** There are 360° in a circle, so subtracting the given degrees from 360° leaves Ajay with 120°. The full 360° represents 90 goals and 360° ÷ 90 = 4°, so every 4° represents 1 goal. Divide Ajay's 120° by 4° to find 30 goals.

2 $\frac{1}{6}$ Carl scored $\frac{60}{360} = \frac{1}{6}$.

3 **20%** Evie scored $\frac{72}{360} = \frac{1}{5} = \frac{20}{100}$.

4 **7** Locate the bar that represents 5–9 goals and read off the frequency on the vertical axis.

5 **16** Add the frequency for 0–4 and 5–9 (9 + 7 = 16).

6 **impossible to say** There is not enough information on the chart to show how individual players performed. Although 9 players scored 0–4 goals, we have no idea how that data breaks down.

7 **29** For each of the first 5 minutes, locate the number of goals from the vertical axis and add them up (2 + 5 + 3 + 8 + 11 = 29).

8 **17th–19th minutes** Read the data from the graph from 8th–10th minutes and 17th–19th minutes (see Q7). 13 + 18 + 17 = 48; 15 + 14 + 20 = 49)

9 **3** There are 6 games, so for the same number of goals to be scored in each one, the total goals must be a multiple of 6. No games scored exactly 6 or 12 but at the 9th minute there were 18 goals scored. This must mean that 3 goals were scored in each of the 6 matches because 6 × 3 = 18.

10 Evie scored 20% of the total goals. 20% of 90 is 18. Carl and Bella both scored $\frac{1}{6}$ of the goals. $\frac{1}{6}$ of 90 = 15. So all three of these players' goals need to be added to the 15–19 section on the graph.

Goals scored by all players

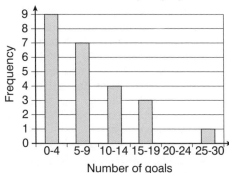

Number of goals

11 **6** There are a total of 24 frequencies, so divide that by the number of teams to find the number of players in each team (24 ÷ 4 = 6).

12 **false** Daisy scored 12 goals, so one-third would be 4 goals. In the first minute of the matches, there were only 2 goals scored, so Daisy could not have scored 4 in the first minute.

Focus Test 12: Mean, median, mode, range and probability
(pages 23–24)

1 **23** The mode is the most common number, and 23 appears on the chart more times than any other number.

2 **26** To find the mean, add up the numbers and then divide by the number of numbers ($28 + 32 + 27 + 25 + 18 + 23 + 29 = 182$; $182 \div 7 = 26$).

3 **£1.35** To find the median, put the numbers in order from smallest to largest and find the middle number (£1.20, £1.25, £1.30, **£1.35,** £1.40, £1.40, £1.55).

4 **Saturday** To find the range, subtract the smallest number from the largest number. The range on Saturday is $34 - 19 = 15$, while the range on Sunday is $32 - 18 = 14$.

5–6 **16, 17** Use logic to work out possible numbers. First, look at the range. The range is 12 and the lowest number of ice creams sold is 15. If that is the bottom value in the range, then 27 is the highest ($15 + 12 = 27$). Both these numbers already appear on the chart. The missing numbers must not be lower than 15 nor higher than 27, so the possible numbers are 15, 16, 17, 18, 19, 20, 21, 22, 23, 24, 25, 26, 27. Next, look at the mean. 7 days × the mean of 19 = 133, so subtracting the numbers already given ($133 - 27 - 20 - 15 - 20 - 18 = 33$) shows that the pair of numbers must add up to 33. The only numbers that are still possible are 15, 16, 17, 18. Now look at the mode. It is 20, and there are already 2 number 20s. The numbers 15 and 18 cannot be used as they already appear once each on the chart. The only possible numbers remaining are 16 and 17.

7 **arrow on the $\frac{1}{2}$ marker** The probability of scoring an even number is the same as scoring an odd number, as half the numbers from 1 to 6 are odd (1, 3, 5) and the other half even (2, 4, 6).

8 **arrow on the first marker after 0** There is a 1 in 6 chance of scoring a number 3. The probability scale is divided into 6 increments, so the first increment represents 1 in 6.

9 **0** As the spinner only has numbers 1 to 6, it is impossible (0) to score a 7.

10 $\frac{5}{9}$ There are 5 odd numbers (1, 3, 5, 7, 9) out of a total of 9.

11 $\frac{1}{3}$ There are 3 cards that are multiples of 3 (3, 6, 9) out of 9 cards, so $\frac{3}{9} = \frac{1}{3}$.

12 **spinning a 2 on the spinner** There is a 1 in 6 chance of spinning a 2 on the spinner and a 1 in 9 change of picking a 2 from the set of digit cards, so the probability is higher on the spinner.

Mixed Paper 1 (pages 25–27)

1 **14510** When rounding a number to the nearest 10, look at the number in the ones column. If it is 4 or below, leave the number in the tens column unchanged. If it is 5 or above, raise the number in the tens column by 1.

2 **14500** When rounding a number to the nearest 100, look at the number in the tens column. If it is 4 or below, leave the number in the hundreds column unchanged. If it is 5 or above, raise the number in the hundreds column by 1.

3 **15000** When rounding a number to the nearest 1000, look at the number in the hundreds column. If it is 4 or below, leave the number in the thousands column unchanged. If it is 5 or above, raise the number in the thousands column by 1.

4 **8470** To solve this, work backwards and reverse the operations. $84.7 \times 100 = 8470$.

5 **>** See Focus test 1, Q1.

1	.	1	0	1
1	.	0	1	1

6–7 Complete the multiplication without the decimal point. Then add up the number of digits after the decimal point in the question and ensure the answer has the same number of digits after the decimal point.

6 **114.52** $409 \times 28 = 11452$ and there are 2 digits after the decimal point in the question (9 and 8), so the answer is 114.52.

7 **1.2544** $196 \times 064 = 12544$ and there are 4 digits after the decimal point in the question (9, 6, 6 and 4), so the answer is 1.2544.

8 **£162** Multiply £13.50 by 12 using the same method as question 6. $1350 \times 12 = 16200$ and there are 2 digits after the decimal point in the question (5 and 0), so the answer is £162.00.

9 **400** Work out the brackets before subtracting 5 ($27 \times 15 = 405$; $405 - 5 = 400$).

10 **860** $33 \times 26 = 858$; $858 + 2 = 860$.

11 **16** See Focus test 3, Q6–7. Factors of 16 are 1, 2, 4, 8, **16** and factors of 48 are 1, 2, 3, 4, 6, 8, 12, **16**, 24, 48.

12 **1, 2, 4, 8, 16, 32, 64, 128** See Focus test 3, Q1.

13 **300** See Focus test 3, Q5. The multiples of 50 include 50, 100, 150, 200, 250, **300** and multiples of 60 include 60, 120, 180, 240, **300**.

14 **3, 13, 23** A prime number is any number that can only be divided by itself and 1. Make a list of the prime numbers below 30: 2, 3, 5, 7, 11, 13, 17, 19, 23, 29. 897 is quite a large number, so start by multiplying the largest three of those ($29 \times 23 = 667$). This is too big, so try other combinations using smaller numbers until finding one that works ($23 \times 13 = 299$; $299 \times 3 = 897$).

15 **53** This number can only be divided by itself and 1.

16 **$1\frac{5}{14}$** See Focus test 4, Q7. $\frac{6}{7} = \frac{36}{42}$; $\frac{5}{6} = \frac{35}{42}$; $\frac{1}{3} = \frac{14}{42}$; $\frac{36}{42} + \frac{35}{42} - \frac{14}{42} = \frac{57}{42} = 1\frac{15}{42} = 1\frac{5}{14}$

17–18 **Year 5 = 300, Year 6 = 450** See Focus test 4, Q5. $2 + 3 = 5$; $750 \div 5 = 150$, so there are 300 points for Year 5 ($150 \times 2 = 300$) and 450 points for Year 6 ($150 \times 3 = 450$).

19–20 Begin with the known fraction, decimal or percentage and work out the missing information from this.

19 **$\frac{3}{10}$ = 0.3 = 30%** $0.3 = 30\% = \frac{30}{100} = \frac{3}{10}$

20 **$\frac{1}{4}$ = 0.25 = 25%** $25\% = 0.25 = \frac{25}{100} = \frac{1}{4}$

21–22 **1024, 2048** See Focus test 5, Q1. The sequence rule is to multiply by 2 each time, so $512 \times 2 = 1024$ and $1024 \times 2 = 2048$.

23–24 **22, 29** See Focus test 5, Q1. The sequence rule is to increase the number added by one each time ($+1, +2, +3, +4$, etc.), so $16 + 6 = 22$ and $22 + 7 = 29$.

25 **512** See Focus test 5, Q11 ($8 \times 8 = 64$; $64 \times 8 = 512$).

26–28 Start by collecting like terms (See Focus test 6, Q3–5), then simplify to find what the letter represents.

26 **7** $6r + 4r = 10r = 70 (\div 10)$ $r = 7$

27 **18** $8s - 3s = 5s = 90 (\div 5)$ $r = 18$

28 **6** $36t \div 4 = 9t$
$9t = 54$; $t = 6$ (divide both sides by 9)

29 **$10n^2$** See Focus test 8, Q1 ($5n \times 2n = 10n^2$).

30 **14n** See Focus test 8, Q2 ($5n + 2n + 5n + 2n = 14n$).

31 **hexagon** A six-sided shape is called a hexagon.

32 **6** The lines of symmetry on a regular shape are equal to the number of sides.

33 **trapezium** A trapezium has one pair of parallel lines.

34 **rhombus** or **parallelogram** A rhombus is a special type of parallelogram that has all four sides the same length.

35 **60°** A regular hexagon is made of equilateral triangles, so each angle of the triangle is 60°.

36–38 See Focus test 8, Q3.

36 **36 cm²** $12 \times 6 \div 2 = 36\,cm^2$

37 **31.5 cm²** $7 \times 9 \div 2 = 31.5\,cm^2$

38 **18 cm²** $8 \times 4.5 \div 2 = 18\,cm^2$

39 **19.5 m²** See Focus test 8, Q1 ($7.8\,m \times 2.5\,m = 19.5\,m^2$).

40 **21** See Focus test 8, Q2. $7.8\,m + 2.5\,m + 7.8\,m + 2.5\,m = 20.6\,m$, so 21 fence panels would be needed to go all of the way round the garden.

41–42 Convert each pair to the same scale to work out the difference between them.

41 **>** $0.8\,m \times 100 = 80\,cm$, and $80\,cm > 75\,cm$

42 **<** $2901\,g \div 1000 = 2.901\,kg$, and $2.901\,kg < 2.91\,kg$

43–44 To compare measurements using different scales, convert each weight to the same scale.

43 **20.1 kg** Converting gives 12 kg (12 000 g), 2.01 kg, 12 kg, 2.1 kg (2100 g), **20.1 kg.**

44 **12 000 g, 12 kg**

45 **2 m** There are approximately 3.3 feet to 1 metre.

46 **30%** The whole pie chart makes up 100% and it has been divided into 10 equal segments, so each segment represents 10%. The pie chart shows 200 sandwiches, so each segment is worth 20 sandwiches. Cheese sandwiches take up 3 segments, so $3 \times 10\% = 30\%$.

47 **40** Chicken sandwiches take up 2 segments of the pie chart, so $2 \times 20 = 40$ sandwiches.

48 **$\frac{1}{5}$** The section for salad is 2 segments out of 10. This is $\frac{2}{10} = \frac{1}{5}$.

49 **20** Cheese and tuna sandwiches together take up 4 segments, while tomato and chicken sandwiches together take up 3 segments. Each segment is worth 20 sandwiches, so there are 20 more cheese and tuna sandwiches.

50 **25%** An extra 40 egg sandwiches would make 60 sandwiches out of 240 total sandwiches sold $\left(\frac{60}{240} = \frac{6}{24} = \frac{1}{4} = \frac{25}{100} = 25\%\right)$.

Mixed Paper 2 (pages 28–31)

1 **3.45** The three-digit number that has the numbers in consecutive order and rounds to 3.5 must be 3.45.

2 **3.05** See Focus test 1, Q1.

3 **100** See Focus test 1, Q9.

4 **10** To multiply a number by 10, move all of the numbers on the decimal grid 1 place to the left.

5 **1000** To divide a number by 1000, move all of the numbers on the decimal grid 3 places to the right.

EXPANDED ANSWERS

Bond Maths Assessment Papers Challenge 10–11+ years

A9

	0.048		
	0.06	**0.8**	
0.3	**0.2**	4	

Divide 0.048 by 0.06 to find 0.8. To do this, make both numbers whole numbers and use long division. Then adjust for the decimal places. Divide 0.06 by 0.3 to find 0.2. Divide 0.8 by 0.2 to find 4.

9 **6900** 12 × 575 = 6900

10 **147.5 km** 29.5 × 5 = 147.5 km

11–12 **8, 9** Divide 288 by 7, 8 and 9 to find which of these numbers divides exactly into it.

13–15 **30, 42, 210** See Focus test 3, Q5.
Multiples of 5: 5, 10, 15, 20, 25, **30,** 35, 40, 45, 50, 55, 60, 65, 70, 75, 80, 85, 90, 95, 100, 105, 110, 115, 120, 125, 130, 135, 140, 145, 150, 155, 160, 165, 170, 175, 180, 185, 190, 195, 200, 205, **210**
Multiples of 6: 6, 12, 18, 24, **30,** 36, **42,** 48, 54, 60, 66, 72, 78, 84, 90, 96, 102, 108, 114, 120, 126, 132, 138, 144, 150, 156, 162, 168, 174, 180, 186, 192, 198, 204, **210**
Multiples of 7: 7, 14, 21, 28, 35, **42,** 49, 56, 63, 70, 77, 84, 91, 98, 105, 112, 119, 126, 133, 140, 147, 154, 161, 168, 175, 182, 189, 196, 203, **210**

16–17 Convert metres into centimetres (2 m = 200 cm) and form a fraction with 200 as the denominator, then simplify.

16 $\frac{20}{200}$ or $\frac{1}{10}$

17 $\frac{50}{200}$ or $\frac{1}{4}$

18 $\frac{40}{200}$ or $\frac{1}{5}$

19 **6 litres** Orange cordial to spring water is 1 part to 5 so, if there is 1 litre of orange cordial, there are 5 litres of sparkling water (1 + 5 = 6 litres of orange drink).

20 **15 litres** Fruit Bowl is 2 parts orange drink to 3 parts fresh pineapple juice. 6 litres of orange drink = 2 parts, so 9 litres of fresh pineapple juice = 3 parts (If 6 litres = 2, then 3 litres = 1 part, so 3 litres × 3 parts = 9 litres). The total amount of Fruit Bowl is 6 litres + 9 litres = 15 litres.

21 **64** See Focus test 5, Q11 (4 × 4 = 16; 16 × 4 = 64).

22–23 **–33, 3** The rule for the sequence is to add 12 each time. Reverse this to find the first missing number (–21 – 12 = –33) and add 12 to the previous number to find the second (–9 + 12 = 3).

24–25 **2, –16** The rule for the sequence is to subtract 6 each time (8 – 6 = 2 and –10 – 6 = –16).

26 **18** See Focus test 5, Q5–6. There are 13 numbers between –13 and 0, and 5 numbers between 0 and 5 (13 + 5 = 18).

27 **13** Work out the difference between the number of cubes in each shape in the sequence. From 4 to 7 = +3, so add 3 each time (10 + 3 = 13).

28 **3n + 1** As the sequence is +3 each time, it is the first part of the formula (3n). If n = 1, then 3n means 3 × 1 = 3. The first shape has 4 cubes. To get from 3 to 4, add 1. This is the final part of the formula: 3n + 1.

29 **31** Use the formula, replacing n with 10 (3 × 10 + 1 = 31).

30–31 **ab + c, (a × b) + c** When letters are placed together, it means to multiply them.

32 **right angle** A right angle is exactly 90°.

33 **acute** An acute angle is less than 90°.

34 **reflex** A reflex angle is more than 180°.

35 **obtuse** An obtuse angle is more than 90° but less than 180°.

36 **sometimes** An isosceles triangle has two angles the same. If the isosceles triangle has one 90° and two 45° angles, it is both an isosceles and a right-angled triangle.

37 **105 mm** Round 103.5 mm up to the nearest 5 mm.

38 **600 mm** Round 599 mm up to the nearest 5 mm.

39 **4.5 cm** Subtract first (105 mm – 60 mm = 45 mm) and then convert into centimetres (45 mm = 4.5 cm).

40 **37 000 ml** Mixed paper 1, Q43–44. Converting these all to ml gives 370 ml, 3070 ml (3.07 l), 7300 ml, 37 000 ml, 7300 ml (7.3 l).

41 **50 miles** There are 1.6 kilometres to 1 mile.

42–44 **(0, 1) (–1, 6) (2, 3)**

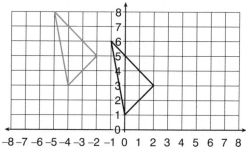

45 **rotation** See Focus test 10, Q1–3. Shape B has been rotated 180°.

46 **translation** See Focus test 10, Q1. This new shape has moved down and to the right.

47 **13°C** See Focus test 12, Q2. 6°C + 7°C + 9°C + 12°C + 15°C + 19°C + 21°C + 20°C + 17°C + 13°C + 9°C + 8°C = 156°C and 156°C ÷ 12 = 13°C

48 **12.5°C** See Focus test 12, Q3. When these numbers are placed in order, there are two numbers in the middle (6, 7, 8, 9, 9, **12, 13,** 15, 17, 19, 20, 21). Add them together and divide by 2 to find the median (12°C + 13°C = 25; 25 ÷ 2 = 12.5°C).

49 **9°C** See Focus test 12, Q1. There are more occurrences of 9°C than any other number.

50 **15°C** See Focus test 12, Q4. 21°C – 6°C = 15°C

Mixed Paper 3 (pages 32–35)

1–3 See Focus test 5, Q1.

1 **1.02** The rule of the sequence is to add 0.2 each time, and 0.82 + 0.2 = 1.02.

2 **0.875** The rule of the sequence is to add 0.125 each time, and 0.75 + 0.125 = 0.875.

3 **1** The rule of the sequence is to multiply by 10 each time, and 0.1 × 10 = 1.

4 $\frac{7}{10}$**, 7 tenths** or **0.7** The 7 is in the tenths column.

5 **843** Use 'bus stop' division to divide 24 into 20 232.

```
              8   4   3
   24 |  2   0   2   3   2
         1   9   2
             1   0   3
                 9   6
             _____
                 7   2
                 7   2
             _____
                     0
```

6 **5.8 kg** Multiply 1.45 kg by 4.

7 **234** Write out each part of the multiplication, then work logically (18 × (11 + 2) = 18 × 13 = 234).

8 **£6426** See Focus test 2, Q2.

```
          1   8   9
   X          3   4
          7   5   6
      5   6   7   0
   _____
   6   4   2   6
```

9 **57** Work out 3648 divided by 8 to find Jyoti's original number (3648 ÷ 8 = 456), then divide by 8 again to find the answer (456 ÷ 8 = 57).

10–12 **2, 4, 7** The factors of 28 are 1, 2, 4, 7, 14, 28 but only 2, 4 and 7 appear on the list.

13 **36** The pairs of factors work in reverse order, so 1 × ?, 2 × 18, 3 × 12, 4 × 9 and then 6 on its own indicates a square number (6 × 6). All of these factor pairs result in 36.

14–15 **27, 57** See Mixed paper 1, Q14. 27 is a multiple of 3 and 9 and 57 is a multiple of 3 and 19. Add up the digits of a number and if the result is divisible by 3, that number is a multiple of 3.

16–17 To convert a fraction to a decimal, use equivalent fractions to make the denominator 100, place the decimal on a decimal grid and write it in its lowest terms. If the numerator is greater than 100, there will be whole numbers before the decimal point.

16 **1.7** $\frac{34}{20} = \frac{170}{100} = 1.70$

17 **0.25** $\frac{9}{36} = \frac{1}{4} = \frac{25}{100} = 0.25$

18–20 Convert each score so that it is out of 100. The numerator is then a percentage.

18 **74%** $\frac{37}{50} = \frac{74}{100} = 74\%$

19 **72%** $\frac{18}{25} = \frac{72}{100} = 72\%$

20 **40%** $\frac{8}{20} = \frac{40}{100} = 40\%$

21 **17°C** There are 12 degrees from 0°C to 12°C and 5 degrees from –5°C to 0°C, so the difference is 17°C (12°C + 5°C = 17°C).

22 **16°C** There are 8 degrees from 0°C to 8°C and 8 degrees from –8°C to 0°C, so the difference is 16°C (8°C + 8°C = 16°C).

23–24 **121, 169** See Focus test 5, Q1. This sequence is square numbers, so the missing numbers are 10² = 100 and 12² = 144.

25–29 See Focus test 6, Q10–11.

25 **4** Add 31 to both sides to get rid of –31; this gives $8v = 32$. Divide by 8 to find v.

26 **6** Subtract 9 from both sides to get rid of 9; this gives $3w = 18$. Divide by 3 to find w.

27 **7** Add 12 to both sides to get rid of –12 and collect like terms; this gives $5q = 35$. Divide by 5 to find q.

28 **4** Solve 6², then subtract 8 from both sides to get rid of 8; this gives $7p = 28$. Divide by 7 to find p.

29 **8** 5.6 – 4.8 = 0.8, so $\frac{r}{10} = 0.8$. Now multiply both sides by 10 to get rid of the fraction and find r.

30 **25 cm** The sides of a square are equal in length, so the area is a square number. See Focus test 8, Q11. For 625 cm², 10 × 10 = 100, which is too low, and 20 × 20 = 400, which is also too low. 30 × 30 = 900, which is too high. 25 × 25 = 625 and this is the correct answer.

31 **20.25 m²** To find the length of the square's sides, divide the perimeter by 4 (18 m ÷ 4 = 4.5 m). Then square this number to find the area (4.5 m × 4.5 m = 20.25 m²).

EXPANDED ANSWERS

Bond Maths Assessment Papers Challenge 10–11⁺ years

32–33 See Focus test 8, Q3.

32 **7.5 cm²** 2.5 cm × 6 cm = 15 cm and 15 cm ÷ 2 = 7.5 cm²

33 **13 cm²** 6.5 cm × 4 cm = 26 cm and 26 cm ÷ 2 = 13 cm²

34–35 Use the same formula for finding the area of a triangle, replacing the parts of the equation with the measurements given. Then work in reverse to find the height.

34 **7.8 cm** 6.5 cm × H ÷ 2 = 25.35 cm²; 25.35 cm² × 2 = 50.7 cm²; 50.7 cm² ÷ 6.5 cm = 7.8 cm

35 **3.2 cm** 5.4 cm × B ÷ 2 = 8.64 cm²; 8.64 cm² × 2 = 17.25 cm²; 17.25 cm² ÷ 5.4 cm = 3.2 cm

36–37 To find the percentage of a number, divide the number by 100 and then multiply by the percentage. Convert the scale if necessary.

36 **0.75 litres** 3 litres ÷ 100 = 0.03 litres; 0.03 litres × 25% = 0.75 litres or 750 ml

37 **1120 g** 5.6 kg ÷ 100 = 0.056 kg; 0.056 kg × 20% = 1.12 kg or 1120 g

38–40 Convert the lengths into the same scale before finding the mean, median and range (4236 m ÷ 1000 = 4.236 km, 316 800 cm ÷ 100 000 = 3.168 km, 4 938 000 ÷ 1 000 000 = 4.938 km, 5800 m ÷ 1000 = 5.8 km, 54 300 cm ÷ 10 000 = 0.543 km).

38 **4 km** See Focus test 12, Q2. 4.236 + 5.08 + 3.168 + 4.938 + 4.235 + 5.8 + 0.543 = 28 km; 28 km ÷ 7 = **4 km**

39 **4.236 km** See Focus test 12, Q3. In order, the measurements are 0.543, 3.168, 4.235, **4.236**, 4.938, 5.08, 5.8.

40 **5.257 km** See Focus test 12, Q4. 5.8 km – 0.543 km = **5.257 km**

41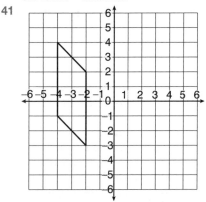

42 **parallelogram** A parallelogram has 2 sets of parallel lines: 2 longer sides of equal length and 2 shorter sides of equal length.

43–45 **(0, –1) (5, –1) (3, –3)** The easiest way to rotate a shape is to use a piece of tracing paper and to trace the shape. Then hold the corner at point –2, –3 and rotate the paper 90° clockwise.

46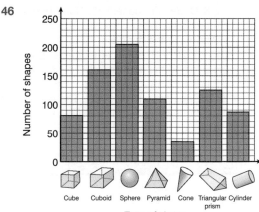

Number of shapes / Type of shape
(Cube, Cuboid, Sphere, Pyramid, Cone, Triangular prism, Cylinder)

47 **more with 6 faces** Cubes and cuboids have 6 faces. There are 80 cubes and 160 cuboids, which makes 240 in total. Square-based pyramids and triangular prisms have 5 faces. There are 110 pyramids and 125 triangular prisms, which makes 235 in total.

48 **cube, prism** There are 80 cubes and 125 prisms, which add up to 205. This is equal to the number of spheres.

49 **20%** $\frac{160}{800} = \frac{20}{100} = 20\%$

50 **120** The cylinders (85) and cone (35) have a curved edge (85 + 35 = 120).

Mixed Paper 4 (pages 36–39)

1 **6.05** When rounding a number to the nearest hundredth, look at the number in the thousandths column. If it is 4 or below, leave the number in the hundredths column unchanged. If it is 5 or above, raise the number in the hundredths column by 1.

2 **14** When rounding a number to the nearest whole number, look at the number in the tenths column. If it is 4 or below, leave the number in the units column unchanged. If it is 5 or above, raise the number in the units column by 1.

3 **117.0** See Focus test 1, Q4–6.

4 $\frac{5}{10}$, **5 tenths or 0.5** Locate the digit and check which decimal position it is in. It is in the tenths column.

5 **337.64** See Mixed paper 2, Q4.

6 **4800** Multiply the number of pencils in a packet by the number of packets to a box and the number of boxes to a container to find the total number of pencils (12 × 16 × 25 = 4800).

7 **40p** or **£0.40** Divide the cost of one container by the total number of pencils to find the individual cost (£1920.00 ÷ 4800 = £0.40 or 40p).

8 **7560 pens** Multiply the number of pens in a tub by the number of tubs in a box and the number of boxes in a container, then multiply the result by 2 to find the total number of pens bought (14 × 15 × 18 × 2 = 7560 pens).

9 **£2646** Multiply the total number of pens by 35p to find the cost for 2 containers (7560 × 35 = 264 600p = £2646.00)

10 **101 928**

```
        3   2   8   8
    ×           3   1
    ─────────────────
        3   2   8   8
    9   8   6   4   0
    ─────────────────
1   0   1   9   2   8
```

11–12 **3, 7** If the digits of a number added together are in the 3 times table, the number can be divided by 3, so 5166 ÷ 3 = 1722. Also, 5166 ÷ 7 = 738.

13–14 **5, 8** If a number ends in a 5 or a 0, the number can be divided by 5, so 2560 ÷ 5 = 512. Also, 512 ÷ 8 = 64.

15–17 Questions like this can be solved by turning the figures into a ratio (see Focus test 4, Q4 and Q5). The lengths of Dan's, Kim's and Ali's skipping ropes can be represented by the ratio $\frac{1}{2} : 1 : 1\frac{1}{2}$ and the total length is 6 m. The three parts of the ratio add up to 3 $\left(\frac{1}{2} + 1 + 1\frac{1}{2} = 3\right)$ and 6 m ÷ 3 = 2 m, so each 1 in the ratio represents 2 m.

15 **3 m** $2\,m \times 1\frac{1}{2} = 3\,m$

16 **1 m** $2\,m \times \frac{1}{2} = 1\,m$

17 **2 m** $2\,m \times 1 = 2\,m$

18–19 To convert an improper fraction, divide the numerator by the denominator to find the whole numbers. The remainder is written as a fraction and in its lowest form.

18 $3\frac{1}{3}$ $\frac{30}{9}$ = 30 ÷ 9 = 3 r 3 = $3\frac{3}{9}$ = $3\frac{1}{3}$

19 $4\frac{4}{5}$ $\frac{48}{10}$ = 48 ÷ 10 = $4\frac{8}{10}$ = $4\frac{4}{5}$

20–21 See Focus test 6, Q3–5.

20 **3a^2 + 2c** 3c + 2a^2 + a^2 − c = 3a^2 + 2c

21 **7a − 14** 4(a − 2) + 3a − 6 = 4a − 8 + 3a − 6 = 7a − 14

22–23 See Focus test 6, Q10–11.

22 **y = 2** Subtract 7 from both sides to get rid of the 7; this gives 4y = y + 6. Now subtract y from both sides to get rid of the y; this gives 3y = 6, so divide to find the answer (6 ÷ 3 = 2).

23 **x = 1.5 or $1\frac{1}{2}$** Add 12 to both sides to get rid of −12; this gives 15x = 5x + 15. Now subtract 5x from both sides to get rid of 5x; this gives 10x = 15, so divide to find the answer $\left(15 ÷ 10 = 1.5 \text{ or } 1\frac{1}{2}\right)$.

24 **−2.2** From 6.4 to 4.2 is −2.2 and from 4.2 to 2 is also −2.2, so the rule of the sequence is to subtract 2.2 each time.

25 **+$\frac{1}{8}$** From $\frac{1}{2}\left(=\frac{4}{8}\right)$ to $\frac{5}{8}$ is +$\frac{1}{8}$ and from $\frac{5}{8}$ to $\frac{3}{4}\left(=\frac{6}{8}\right)$ is also +$\frac{1}{8}$, so the rule of the sequence is to add $\frac{1}{8}$ each time.

26–27 **x = 10°, y = 5°** There are 180° in a triangle. Collect like terms to divide into 180° to find the value of x and y. In the first triangle, 10x + 4x + 4x = 18x and 180° ÷ 18x = 10, so x = 10°. In the second triangle, 26y + 5y + 5y = 36y and 180° ÷ 36y = 5, so y = 5°.

28 **144** If the square root is 12, then the square number is 144 (12 × 12 = 144).

29 **6** If r ÷ 2 = 3, then r = 6 (2 × 3 = 6).

30–33 There are 360° in a circle. 360° ÷ 12 hours = 30°. As each hour is worth 30°, it is easy to add together combinations of hours.

30 **120°** From 12 to 4 = 4 hours and 4 × 30° = 120°

31 **30°** From 8 to 9 = 1 hour and 1 × 30° = 30°

32 **180°** From 5 to 11 = 6 hours and 6 × 30° = 180°

33 **4** 90° = 3 hours (3 × 30), so 1 + 3 hours = 4

34–35 See Focus test 8, Q3.

34 **12.5 cm²** The base and the height are both 5 cm, so 5 cm × 5 cm ÷ 2 = 12.5 cm².

35 **16 cm²** The base is 8 cm and the height is 4 cm, so 4 cm × 8 cm ÷ 2 = 16 cm².

36 **135 000 cm³** See Focus test 8, Q7. 90 cm × 30 cm × 50 cm = 135 000 cm³

37 **954 cm²** To find the surface area of a cuboid, find the area of each face and add them together. Working in 3 sets of pairs makes it easier to include each face (2 × 22 × 9 = 396 cm²; 2 × 22 × 9 = 396 cm²; 2 × 9 × 9 = 162 cm²; 396 cm² + 396 cm² + 162 cm² = 954 cm²).

38 **1782 cm³** See Focus test 8, Q7. 22 cm × 9 × 9 = 1782 cm³

39–40 **length = 27 cm, width = 18 cm** Put the information in the form of a ratio (1 : 1.5). The perimeter is made up of 2 lengths and 2 widths, so double the numbers in the ratio (2 : 3). Add together the ratios to make a group (2 + 3 = 5), then divide 900 mm by this group (900 mm ÷ 5 mm = 180 mm). Now multiply this by the individual ratios to find the total width and length (180 mm × 2 = 360 mm and 180 mm × 3 = 540 mm). Divide each by 2 to find the measurement of a single side (2 widths = 360 mm, so each width is 180 mm; 2 lengths = 540 mm, so each length is 270 mm). Finally, convert the answer to centimetres (180 mm = 18 cm; 270 mm = 27 cm).

Ingredient	Imperial	Metric
Flour	14 oz	**390 g**
Butter	7 oz	**195 g**
Sugar	6 oz	**170 g**

Multiply 14 oz by 28 to find 390 g. Multiply 7 oz by 28 to find 196 g. Multiply 6 oz by 28 to find 170 g. Round to the nearest 5 g.

44 **94 g** *or* **95 g** Add up the weight of ingredients and divide by 8. If working in grams, 390 g + 195 g + 170 g = 755; 755 ÷ 8 = 94.375 g, rounded down to 94 g. If working in ounces, 14 oz + 7 oz + 6 oz = 27 oz; 27 oz ÷ 8 = 3.375 oz; 3.375 oz × 28 = 94.5 g, rounded up to 95 g.

45 **24** The whole pie chart represents 360°, so half a circle represents 180°. 180° − 60° = 120° for the 'More than 1 pet' section, which is 8 children. If 8 children = 120°, then 4 children = 60°. The half circle = 12 children, so there are 24 children in the whole class.

46 **30** The circle is divided into 3 equal parts. If $\frac{1}{3}$ = 10 children, there are 30 children in the whole class (3 × 10 = 30).

47 **28** The circle is divided into quarters. If $\frac{1}{4}$ = 7 children, there are 28 children in the whole class (4 × 7 = 28).

48 **21** There are 4 children in Class 4 with only one pet (60° = 4). There are 10 children in Class 5 with only one pet $\left(\frac{1}{3} = 10\right)$. There are 7 children in Class 6 with only one pet. 4 + 10 + 7 = 21 children with only one pet.

49 **5** There are 12 children without a pet in Class 4 (180° = 3 × 4 children). There are 7 children without a pet in Class 6 $\left(\frac{1}{4}\text{ of }28 = 7\right)$ and 12 − 7 = 5.

50 **false** There are 8 children with more than one pet in Class 4 and 10 children with more than one pet in Class 5, so the statement is false.

Mixed Paper 5 (pages 40–43)

1–4 **0.279 < 0.927 < 2.09 < 2.7** See Focus test 1, Q1.

5 **0.36** Find the pairs of digits that total 9, then cross out those that do not round to 0.4 to the nearest 10 (0.18, 0.27, **0.36**, 0.45, 0.54, 0.63, 0.72, 0.81).

6 **31.5 cm** Divide the length by 6 (189 cm ÷ 6 = 31.5 cm).

7 **40** Work out the brackets first (378 ÷ 18 = 21; 21 + 19 = 40).

8 **46** Work out the brackets first (403 ÷ 13 = 31; 31 + 15 = 46).

9 **5** Convert the 2 litres and the 0.4 litres into ml, then divide (2000 ml ÷ 400 ml = 5).

10 **£3.75** Divide £75 by 20 weeks to find the weekly amount saved (£75.00 ÷ 20 = £3.75).

11 **28** 4 × 7 = 28, so these numbers are factors of 28.

12 **39** 13 × 3 = 39, so these numbers are factors of 39.

13 **16** The only type of number that has an odd number of factors is a square number, and 16 is the only square number in the list.

14–15 **756, 252** Multiply 4 × 7 × 9 to find 252. Add multiples of 252 to find 3 × 252 = 756.

16 **3:1** There are 3 spheres to every 1 cube, so the ratio is 3:1.

17 **5** If there are 15 spheres, divide by 3 to find 5.

18–19 **0.8, 0.4** See Mixed paper 3, Q18–20. $\frac{24}{30} = \frac{8}{10}$ = 0.8 and $\frac{28}{70} = \frac{4}{10}$ = 0.4

20–21 To reduce a price by a percentage, divide the original price by 100 and then multiply by the reduction subtracted from 100.

20 **£75** £125 ÷ 100 = £1.25; £1.25 × 60 = £75

21 **£21.25** £25 ÷ 100 = £0.25 × 85 = £21.25

22 **£50.00** The reduced cost is £40 after a reduction of 20%, so £40 is 80% of the original price. Divide £40 by 80 to find 1%, then multiply by 100 to find the original price (£40 ÷ 80 = £0.50; £0.50 × 100 = £50.00).

23 **9** See Focus test 5, Q11. 9 × 9 = 81; 81 × 9 = 729

24 **7** The number of squares increases by 2 each time, so 5 + 2 = 7.

25 **2n − 1** First, work out the difference of the sequence (from 1 to 3 = +2), which is add 2 each time. This is the first part of the formula, so put this number in front of *n* to make 2n. Make *n* 1 (the first term of the sequence). If *n* = 1, then 2n means 2 × 1 = 2. The first pattern has 1 shaded square. To get from 2 (2n = 2 × 1 = 2) to 1, subtract 1. This means that putting − 1 after the 2n is the final part of the formula. The formula is 2n − 1.

26 **15** Use the same formula, replacing *n* with 8 (2n − 1 = 16 − 1 = 15).

27–28 See Focus test 6, Q10–11.

27 **7** Subtract 17 from both sides to get rid of 17; this gives 8e = 56, so divide by 8 to find *e* (56 ÷ 8 = 7).

28 **8** Work out the brackets first (27 ÷ 9 = 3); this gives 4f + 3 = 35. Now subtract 3 from both sides to get rid of 3; this gives 4f = 32, so divide by 4 to find *f* (32 ÷ 4 = 8).

29–31 A whole circle has 360° and this is divided into 12 hours, making each hour worth 30°.

29 **6** 180° ÷ 30 = 6, so the time would be 6 o'clock.

30 **1** 30° would be one hour, so the time would be 1 o'clock.

31 **5** 150° ÷ 30 = 5, so the time would be 5 o'clock.

32 **126 m²** See Focus test 8, Q1. 8.4 × 15 = 126 m²

33–34 Divide each shape into a rectangle and a triangle. Find the area of each part, then add them together.

33 **36 cm²** The rectangle is 4 cm × 6 cm = 24 cm². The triangle is 6 cm × 4 cm ÷ 2 = 12 cm², so 24 cm² + 12 cm² = 36 cm².

34 **49 cm²** The rectangle is 5 cm × 7 cm = 35 cm². The triangle is 7 cm × 4 cm ÷ 2 = 14 cm², so 35 cm² + 14 cm² = 49 cm².

35 **147 cm** Divide the volume by the base to find the height (5292 cm³ ÷ 36 cm² = 147 cm).

36 **1680 g or 1.68 kg** Top Cat weighs 4 kg, so divide this by 500 g (4000 g ÷ 500 g = 8) to find that Top Cat needs 8 × 30 g = 240 g per day. In a week, he would eat 240 g × 7 days = 1680 g.

37 **2 weeks** Princess weighs 6 kg, so divide this by 500 g (6000 g ÷ 500 g = 12) to find that Princess needs 12 × 30 g = 360 g per day. In a week, she would eat 360 g × 7 = 2520 g (2.52 kg). Divide the 5.5 kg bag by 2.52 kg to see that a bag will last roughly 2 weeks.

38 **71.5 kg** There are 52 weeks in a year, so divide 52 by 4 to work out how many bags are needed for the year. 52 ÷ 4 = 13. Each bag is 5.5 kg so 13 × 5.5 kg = 71.5 kg.

39 **16 bags of food** 1.7 kg × 52 = 88.4 kg of food needed in a year. Divide this by the weight of the bags (88.4 kg ÷ 5.5 kg = 16 to the nearest whole number). So 16 bags of food would be needed.

40–41 To compare, work out the cost of each cereal per 1 kg. Box A: 4 × 250 g = 1 kg; 4 × 42p = 168p per kg; Box B: 2 × 500 g = 1 kg; 2 × 57p = 114p per kg; Box C: 99p per kg; Box D: £1.20 per 1.2 kg so divide £1.20 by 1.2; £1.00 per kg.

40 **C**

41 **A**

42 **(2, −3)** See Focus test 10, Q3.

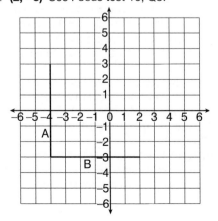

43 **perpendicular** A perpendicular line forms a 90° angle with another line.

44 **(2, −3)** A square has all sides of equal length.

45 **(6, 16)** The x-axis for the top right corner of the triangle is 14 and the mid-point is 10, so to find the missing x-axis angle, subtract 10 from 14 to find 4 and subtract this from the mid-point (10 − 4 = 6) to find the first coordinate. The y-axis will remain the same as the top right corner of the triangle, which is 16.

46 **14** See Focus test 12, Q4. 33 − 19 = 14

47 **26** See Focus test 12, Q2. 28 + 33 + 27 + 19 + 25 + 24 = 156; 156 ÷ 6 = 26

48 $\frac{4}{5}$ Probability is out of 1 whole, so if there is a $\frac{1}{5}$ chance of winning a prize, then there must be a $\frac{4}{5}$ chance of not winning a prize.

49 $\frac{5}{6}$ There are 50 beads that are not yellow (12 + 18 + 20 = 50), so non-yellow beads make up $\frac{50}{60}$ which is equivalent to $\frac{5}{6}$.

50 $\frac{3}{10}$ The fraction for a blue bead is 18 out of 60 and $\frac{18}{60} = \frac{3}{10}$.

Mixed Paper 6 (pages 44–47)

1 **×** The second number is larger, so it must be multiplied.

2 **×** The second number is larger, so it must be multiplied.

3 **÷** The second number is smaller, so it must be divided.

4–5 **6.8, 3.2** The answer is between 21 and 22. Use approximation, look for possible numbers that multiply to make a similar number. 7 × 3 = 21, so try multiplying 7.2 or 6.8 by 3.2 or 3.4. 9.7 is close to 10 and there is nothing close to 2 to multiply that by so it can be excluded.

6 **15** Multiply both numbers by 10 to work in whole numbers (60 ÷ 4 = 15).

7 **0.9** Think of how many times 8 goes into 72, then divide by 10 (72 ÷ 8 = 9; 9 ÷ 10 = 0.9).

8 **62 500** See Mixed paper 1, Q2.

9 **1324.577** When rounding a number to the nearest thousandth, look at the number in the ten-thousandths column. If it is 4 or below, leave the number in the thousandths column unchanged. If it is 5 or above, raise the number in the thousandths column by 1. If the number is already a 9, put a zero in the column and raise the hundredth column by 1. 1324.576**98** = 1324.577

10 **5 140 000** When rounding a number to the nearest thousand, look at the number in the hundreds column. If it is a 4 or below, leave the number in the thousands column

Bond Maths Assessment Papers Challenge 10–11⁺ years

unchanged. If it is a 5 or above, raise the number in the thousands column by one. The remaining numbers to the right up to the decimal point, need a zero in the column. If the number is already a 9, put a zero in the column and raise the ten thousands column by 1. 5 139 768.24 = 5 140 000

11 **always** All square numbers have an odd number of factors as their root is multiplied by itself.

12 **83** See Mixed paper 1, Q14.

13 **81** See Focus test 5, Q1. 9 × 9 = 81

14 **84** All even numbers divide by 2, so 80, 82 and 84 are possible answers. When a number's digits are added up, if they are divisible by three, then the original number is a multiple of 3. 8 + 4 = 12, which can be divided by 3.

15 **8 cm** If 2 cm = 3 m, then 12 m ÷ 3 = 4 and 4 × 2 cm = 8 cm.

16 $\frac{3}{7}$ **of 21** To find a fraction of a number, divide the number by the denominator and multiply the answer by the numerator (24 ÷ 8 = 3 and 3 × 5 = 15; 18 ÷ 3 = 6 and 6 × 2 = 12; 25 ÷ 5 = 5 and 5 × 2 = 10; 21 ÷ 7 = 3 and 3 × 3 = 9. It is now possible to select the lowest number.

17 **0.07** To compare the size of decimal numbers, place them on a decimal grid and work from far left to right to find the smallest to largest.

U	.	t	h
0	.	2	7
0	.	0	7
0	.	2	
0	.	7	2

18 $\frac{27}{63}$ To compare fractions, place them in their lowest form $\left(\frac{40}{56} = \frac{5}{7}; \frac{8}{14} = \frac{4}{7}; \frac{27}{63} = \frac{3}{7}; \frac{42}{49} = \frac{6}{7}\right)$.

19 **<** To turn 0.2 into a percentage, add a zero in the hundredths column (0.20 = 20%).

20–21 Work out both elements each side of the missing operator before comparing.

20 **=** $4^2 \times 3^2 = 16 \times 9 = 144$ and $12^2 \div 1^2 = 144 \div 1 = 144$, so the two sides are equal.

21 **<** $5^3 + 11^2 = 125 + 121 = 246$ and $8^2 \times 2^2 = 64 \times 4 = 256$, so the left-hand side is smaller.

22 **43** The square root of 100 is 10 (10 × 10 = 100) and 10 + 33 = 43.

23 **16, 64** List the square numbers up to 80 (1, 4, 9, 16, 25, 36, 49, 64) and then find the two that add up to 80 (64 + 16 = 80).

24 **($b \times b$) ÷ 2** The area of a triangle is base × height ÷ 2, so ($b \times b$) ÷ 2 is the correct option.

25 **2b + c** To find the perimeter, add up each side. That gives $b + b + c$, which simplifies to $2b + c$.

26 **isosceles** The triangle has two sides the same, so it is an isosceles triangle.

27 **45°** There are 180 degrees in a triangle and the top angle is a right angle, which is 90°. To find y, subtract 90° from 180°, then divide the answer by 2 (180° – 90° = 90°; 90° ÷ 2 = 45°).

28 **5** Diagonal lines can be drawn from any angle to another as long as the angles are not next to each other.

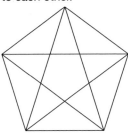

	Shape name	No. of faces	No. of corners	No. of edges
29–32	Tetrahedron	**4**	4	6
	Cuboid	6	8	**12**
	Square-based pyramid	5	**5**	8
	Triangular prism	5	6	**9**

33 **C** For a shape to be the net of a closed cube, there must be a top and bottom, a front and a back, and a left and a right. In each of these pairs, the two faces must be opposite each other. Begin with any face and mark out these opposites. Shape C does not make a cube.

34

35–36 **length = 80 cm, width = 40 cm** Find a pair of numbers that will multiply to 32, where the one number is double the size of the other. 4 × 8 = 32 and 4 × 2 = 8, so 40 cm × 80 cm = 3200 cm².

37 **7700 cm²** Add 30 cm to both the length and the width as there is 15 cm extra on each of the four sides. 40 + 30 = 70 and 80 + 30 = 110, so the area of the tablecloth is 70 × 110 = 7700 cm².

38 **576 cm³** Use the area to find the measurement of the missing side. 48 cm² ÷ 6 cm = 8 cm, so the missing measurement is 8 cm.

A16

Then find the volume by multiplying the length × the height × the depth ($12 \times 6 \times 8 = 576\,cm^3$).

39 isosceles The triangle has two angles the same, so it is an isosceles triangle.

40 1 The triangle has one vertical line of symmetry through the centre.

41–43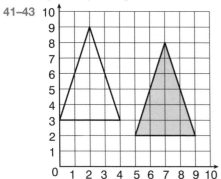

44 translation See Focus test 10, Q1. This triangle has been moved up and to the left.

45 10 Locate 16 km along the horizontal axis. Follow the line up until it connects to the graph line. Follow this point to the vertical axis to read off the miles.

46 45 Locate 28 miles along the vertical axis. Follow the line across until it connects to the graph line. Follow this point down to the horizontal axis to read off the kilometres.

47 37 Locate 23 miles along the vertical axis. Follow the line across until it connects to the graph line. Follow this point down to the horizontal axis to read off the kilometres.

48 20 miles Locate 30 km along the horizontal axis and follow the line up until it connects to the graph line. Follow this point to the vertical axis to find that 30 km is less than 20 miles.

49 Yes Locate 15 miles along the vertical axis. Follow the line across until it connects to the graph line. Follow this point down to the horizontal axis to find that 22 km is less than 15 miles, so he will have enough fuel.

50 30 Locate 50 km along the horizontal axis and follow the line up until it connects to the graph line. Follow this point left to work out that it is just over 30 miles, so to the nearest 10 mph this is 30 mph.

Mixed Paper 7 (pages 48–51)

1–4 See Focus test 1, Q4–6.
1 0.7
2 2.4
3 10.2
4 96.5
5 8 m Multiply 0.08 by 100 to find the height of the wall ($0.08\,m \times 100 = 8\,m$).

6 8832 To find a product, multiply the numbers together ($384 \times 23 = 8832$).

7 £11.20 Divide £8.40 by 6 to find the cost of one plate, then multiply this number by 8 to find the total cost for eight plates ($£8.40 \div 6 = £1.40$; $£1.40 \times 8 = £11.20$).

8–10 **45, 54, 55** The last number must be 55 as it is in the 5 times table and both digits are the same. The first number could be 12, 23, 34 or 45, as all of these are under 50 and have digits that are consecutive numbers. The second number is the reverse of the first but is greater than 40, so reverse the numbers on the list and cross off any that are under 40 (~~21~~, ~~32~~, 43, 54). This shows that the first and second numbers are either 34 and 43 or 45 and 54. Divide the product by the third number (55) and then divide the answer by 34 to see if it works ($133\,650 \div 55 = 2430$; $2430 \div 34 = 71.470$). The answer is not a whole number, so the missing pair of numbers must be 45 and 54 ($2430 \div 45 = 54$).

11–15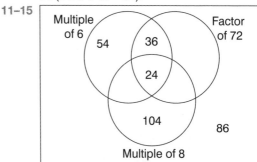

24 is a factor of 72 and a multiple of both 6 and 8, so it fits in the centre area common to all three circles. **36** is a factor of 72 and a multiple of 6, so it fits in the area common to both of these circles. **54** is only a multiple of 6, so it fits in the far left. **86** is neither a factor of 72 nor a multiple of 6 or 8, so it fits outside of the circles. **104** is only a multiple of 8, so it fits in the bottom circle only.

16–17 Convert Jet's pizza into grams so that each pizza has the same scale.

16 Jet = 375 g, Esosa = 450 g For each pizza, find the weight of a single piece and then multiply by the number of slices eaten. For Jet's pizza, this is $1500\,g \div 8 = 187.5\,g$ per piece and $187.5\,g \times 2 = 375\,g$ eaten. For Esosa's pizza, this is $750\,g \div 5 = 150\,g$ per piece and $150\,g \times 3 = 450\,g$ eaten.

17 Jet One piece of Jet's pizza weighs 187.5 g, so add this to his total ($375\,g + 187.5\,g = 562.5\,g$).

18–19 See Mixed paper 3, Q18–20.

18 **25%** $\frac{24}{96} = \frac{1}{4} = \frac{25}{100} = 25\%$

19 **30%** $\frac{45}{150} = \frac{3}{10} = \frac{30}{100} = 30\%$

20 **24** There are a total of 60 children (32 + 28 = 60). Divide the children into groups of 5 and multiply by 2 to find the total number of adults (60 ÷ 5 = 12; 12 × 2 = 24).

21–22 **3, 4** Work out 5^2 (5 × 5 = 25), then list the square numbers that are less than 25: 1, 4, 9, 16. Find two of these numbers that add up to 25 (9 + 16 = 25) and put their square roots into the equation ($3^2 + 4^2 = 5^2$).

23–24 See Focus test 5, Q1.

23 **343** The sequence is descending cubed numbers from 10^3 to 4^3. The missing number is 7^3 and 7 × 7 × 7 = 343.

24 **256** The given numbers are descending squares of even numbers from 14^2 to 4^2. The missing number at the beginning is 16^2 and 16 × 16 = 256.

25 **2(w + l)** The perimeter is the sum of the 2 lengths and the 2 widths, and this equation is equal to 2w + 2l.

26 **23 cm** The area of a rectangle is the length × width, so divide each side of this equation by 15 to leave 23 = l.

27–29 See Focus test 6, Q10–11.

27 **4** Divide each side by 4 to get rid of 4; this gives $m^2 = 16$, so find the root of 16 to get rid of the squared number and find m = 4.

28 **6** Divide each side by 3 to get rid of 3; this gives $n^2 = 36$, so find the root of 36 to get rid of the squared number and find n = 6.

29 **5** Add 15 to both sides to get rid of –15; this gives $4c^2 = 100$, so divide each side by 4 to get rid of 4. This gives $c^2 = 25$, so find the root of 25 to get rid of the squared number and find c = 5.

30 **square-based pyramid**

31 **triangular prism**

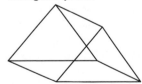

32

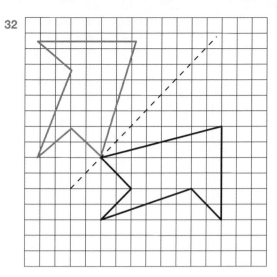

33–35 **angle x = 110°, angle y = 30°, angle z = 230°** The angles of a four-sided shape add up to 360°. For Shape 1, subtract the two 90° angles and the 70° angle to find x (360° – 90° – 90° – 70° = 110°). For Shape 2, subtract the two 120° angles and the 90° angle to find y (360° – 120° – 120° – 90° = 30°). For Shape 3, subtract the two 45° angles and the 40° angle to find z (360° – 45° – 45° – 40° = 230°).

36–39

Gift box shape	Length of lid	Width of lid	Area of lid	Height of box	Volume of box
cube	**17 cm**	17 cm	289 cm²	17 cm	**4913 cm³**
cuboid	9.5 cm	8 cm	**76 cm²**	115 cm	8740 cm³

In a cube, all the edges are the same length so, if the width is 17 cm, the length must also be 17 cm. Multiply length × width × height to find the volume (17 × 17 × 17 = 4913 cm³). For the cuboid box, multiply the length of the lid by the width to find the area of the lid (9.5 cm × 8 cm = 76 cm²). Divide the volume by the length and then by the width to find the height of the box (8740 cm³ ÷ 9.5 cm = 920 cm²; 920 cm² ÷ 8 = 115 cm). Or you could divide the volume by the area of the lid (8740 ÷ 76 = 115).

40 **765 cm²** The square base is 15 cm × 15 cm, so its area is 225 cm² (15 × 15 = 225). The area of each triangle is 135 cm² (18 cm × 15 cm ÷ 2 = 135 cm²). Add one base and four triangles to find the total area (225 cm² + (4 × 135 cm²) = 765 cm²).

41 **1.155 kg** Convert 405 g to kg (405 g = 0.405 kg) and then subtract 0.405 kg from 1.56 kg.

42 **50 inches** There are approximately 2.5 cm to 1 inch, so inches are longer than centimetres.

43 **1400 g** Convert the kilograms to grams, then complete the division (12.6 kg × 1000 = 12 600 g; 12 600 g ÷ 9 = 1400 g).

44 **550 cm** Convert the metres to centimetres, then complete the division (44 m × 100 = 4400 cm; 4400 cm ÷ 8 = 550 cm).

45 **9 km** Locate 10:30 am along the Time axis and trace the line up until it touches the dotted graph line for Sam. Follow this point left to read the distance on the Distance axis.

46 **Sam** Look at the finishing time at the end of the journey to see that Sam's walk finished before Jo's.

47 **$1\frac{1}{2}$ hours** Look at the dotted line when it is horizontal as this is the time Sam is resting. Add the periods of time together (from 10:30 am to 11:00 am is half an hour and from 12:00 pm to 1:00 pm is 1 hour).

48 **2 km** Subtract Jo's distance at 11:00 am from Sam's distance at the same time (9 km – 7 km = 2 km).

49 **12:15 pm** Find the point where Sam's line is horizontal, showing that he was resting, while Jo's crosses it as it continues to climb. Follow this point straight down to read the time.

50 **5 (km per hour)** Jo walked 30 km and completed it in 6 hours (not including rest time), so 30 km ÷ 6 hours = 5 km per hour.

Mixed Paper 8 (pages 52–55)

1–3 See Mixed paper 4, Q2.
  1 **491**
  2 **27**
  3 **51**
4–5 **163248** Begin by listing the possible options for the first double-digit number, which has no repeated digits: 10, 12, 13, 14, 15, 16, 17. Then double each number and cross out any number pairs that share a digit in common: 10 (20), 12 (24), 13 (26), 14 (28), 15 (30), 16 (32), 17 (34). Now take the remaining pairs and multiply the first number by 3, crossing out any that share a digit in common: 13 (26, 39), 14 (28, 42), 15 (30, 45), 16 (32, 48), 17 (34, 51). Only one set of numbers remains so the secret code is 163248.

  6 **63 full cartons, 4 eggs left over** 760 ÷ 12 = 63.33, so there are 63 full cartons. 12 × 63 = 756 and 760 – 754 = 4, so there are 4 eggs left over.

  7 **391** Subtract 15 + 29 from 15 × 29 (435 – 44 = 391).

8–10 The 6 possible numbers that can be made from these digits are 125, 152, 215, 251, 512 and 521.

  8 **251, 521** See Mixed paper 1, Q14. These two numbers have no factors other than 1 and themselves.

  9 **512** See Focus test 5, Q11. 8 × 8 × 8 = 512

 10 **152** Look at the list of factors and take a pair of numbers that are the same distance in from each end of the list (remember that there is a missing factor at the end of the list). Multiply them together (e.g. 2 × 76 = 152, 4 × 38 = 152, 8 × 19 = 152).

 11 **9** See Focus test 3, Q6–7.
    The factors of 18 are 1, 2, 3, 6, **9**, 18.
    The factors of 45 are 1, 3, 5, **9**, 15, 45.

12–13 **2, 3** To find the prime factors of 18, divide 18 by prime numbers until the result is also a prime number (18 ÷ 2 = 9 and 9 ÷ 3 = 3). 3 is a prime number, so 2 and 3 are the prime factors.

14–15 **240** First find the highest common factor of 24 and 36.
    Factors of 24 = 1, 2, 3, 4, 6, 8, **12**, 24
    Factors of 36 = 1, 2, 3, 4, 6, 9, **12**, 18, 36
    Next find the lowest common multiple of 4 and 5 by listing the multiples of each until there is one in common.
    4: 4, 8, 12, 16, **20**
    5: 5, 10, 15, **20**
    Finally, multiply the two numbers together (12 × 20 = 240).

 16 **30 g** Add together the total weight of the ingredients, then divide by 5 (75 g + 50 g + 25 g = 150 g; 150 g ÷ 5 = 30 g).

 17 **$\frac{1}{6}$** The fraction of sugar to the whole biscuit is $\frac{25}{150} = \frac{1}{6}$.

 18 **200 g** 300 g flour is 4 × 75 g, so 4 × 50 g butter will be needed. You could also use ratios to work this out: the ratio of butter to flour is 50 : 75 = 2 : 3. If 300 g of flour is used, 200 g butter will be needed.

 19 **3 : 2** The ratio of flour to butter is 3 : 2. 75 : 50 can be simplified to 3 : 2 by dividing by common factors.

 20 **49** See Focus test 5, Q1. 7 × 7 = 49

 21 **29** See Mixed paper 1, Q14. 29 has no factors other than 1 and itself.

 22 **–3°C** From 11°C to 0°C is 11°C. 14 – 11 = 3, so going down by a further 3°C takes the temperature to –3°C.

23–25 See Focus test 5, Q1.
 23 **13** This sequence is a Fibonnaci sequence where two consecutive terms are added together to make the next term (1 + 1 = 2; 1 + 2 = 3; 2 + 3 = 5; 3 + 5 = 8; 5 + 8 = 13).

24 **2304** The rule of this sequence is to divide by 2 each time, so 4608 ÷ 2 = 2304.

25 **0.3** The rule of this sequence is to divide by 10 each time, so 3 ÷ 10 = 0.3.

26 **(l × w) ÷ 2** The area of a triangle is length × width ÷ 2.

27 **30 cm²** If w = 4 cm and l = 15 cm, the area of the triangle is 4 × 15 ÷ 2 = 30 cm².

28–30 When letters are next to each other, they should be multiplied. Replace the letters with the numbers given, then complete the equation, remembering to work out brackets and squared or cubed numbers first.

28 **5** (7 × 8 − 11) ÷ 9 = (56 − 11) ÷ 9 = 45 ÷ 9 = 5

29 **60** 9² − (8 + 13) = 81 − 21 = 60

30 **18** (16 × 9) ÷ 8 = 144 ÷ 8 = 18

31 **triangular prism**

32 **pentagonal-based pyramid**

33 **triangular based pyramid** *or* **tetrahedron**

34 **8.4** 6 × 14 mm = 84 mm. Divide by 10 to convert mm to cm (84 ÷ 10 = 8.4 cm).

35 **4.86 litres** Convert the measurements to litres, then add them together (0.585 litres + 3.2 litres + 1.075 litres = 4.86 litres).

36 **9 metres** There are roughly 3.3 feet to 1 metre, so 9 metres is longer than 9 feet.

37–39 Convert each length to the measurement given, then add them together.

37 **9365** 470 cm × 10 = 4700 mm and 1.603 m × 1000 = 1603 mm, so 4700 mm + 3062 mm + 1603 mm = 9365 mm.

38 **5156.1** 51 mm ÷ 10 = 5.1 cm and 51 m × 100 = 5100 cm, so 51 cm + 5.1 cm + 5100 cm = 5156.1 cm.

39 **18.59** 879 cm ÷ 100 = 8.79 m and 400 mm ÷ 1000 = 0.4 m, so 8.79 m + 0.4 m + 9.4 m = 18.59 m.

40–43

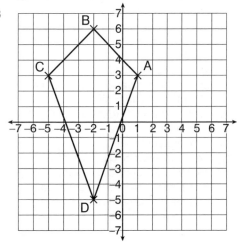

44 **kite** A kite is a four-sided shape with two short sides of equal length that are next to each other and two long sides of equal length that are also next to each other.

45–50 In these questions, probability is expressed on a scale that goes from 0 (impossible) to 1 (certain). The scale is divided into 10 segments with 0.5 in the centre.

45 **0.7** There are 7 chances out of 10 possible outcomes for the card to be greater than 35, which is a probability of 0.7.

46 **0.1** Only 1 of the cards shows a square number out of 10 possible outcomes (10 × 10 = 100), so this is a probability of 0.1.

47 **0** There are no cards with odd numbers, so this is a probability of 0.

48 **0.3** There are 3 cards showing a multiple of 3 (30, 60 and 90), out of 10 possible outcomes so this is a probability of 0.3.

49 **1** All of the numbers on the cards are even, so this is a probability of 1.

50 **0.5** There are 5 cards showing a multiple of 4 (20, 40, 60, 80 and 100) out of 10 possible outcomes, so this is a probability of 0.5.

Mixed Paper 9 (pages 56–59)

1 **24.58** See Mixed paper 6, Q17. The winning time is the smallest number.

2–3 See Focus test 1, Q9.

2 **7.0316**

3 **0.594**

4 **8.530** Place the digits in order, starting with the largest, to make the largest possible number.

5 **0.358** Place the digits in order, starting with the smallest, to make the smallest possible number.

6 **19** Divide 1083 by 57 to find the missing number (1083 ÷ 57 = 19).

7 **16** First multiply 7.2 by 100 to find 720, then divide this by 45 (720 ÷ 45 = 16).

8 **£4.45** Divide £22.25 by 5 to find the cost of each ticket (£22.25 ÷ 5 = £4.45).

9–10 **352 × 24 = 8448** Multiply the units to get the final digit (2 × 4 = 8). Now divide 8448 by 24 to find the other missing digit is 5.

11–14

	Square number	Not a square number
Multiple of 7	49	147
Not a multiple of 7	121	128

15–16 See Mixed paper 3, Q18–20.

15 **20%** $\frac{42}{210} = \frac{1}{5} = \frac{20}{100}$ = 20%

16 **85%** $\frac{68}{80} = \frac{17}{20} = \frac{85}{100}$ = 85%

17–18 Add up the total number of vehicles (144 + 36 + 48 + 12 = 240) and set the number of a particular type of vehicle as a fraction of all vehicles.

17 **60%** Cars make up $\frac{144}{240}$ of all vehicles. Use an equivalent fraction to make the denominator 100, then the numerator will be the percentage $\left(\frac{144}{240} = \frac{6}{10} = \frac{60}{100} = 60\%\right)$.

18 $\frac{1}{5}$ $\frac{48}{240}$ of the vehicles are lorries and $\frac{48}{240} = \frac{1}{5}$.

19 **5%** Buses make up $\frac{12}{240}$ of all vehicles and this is equal to 5% $\left(\frac{12}{240} = \frac{1}{20} = \frac{5}{100} = 5\%\right)$.

20 $\frac{3}{4}$ Out of the total Bikes group, bicycles make up $\frac{27}{36} = \frac{3}{4}$.

21 **<** The square root of 36 is 6 and 6 is smaller than 6.3.

22–24 **13, 21, 29** Subtract 5 from 37 to find 32. Divide 32 by the 4 jumps from 5 to 37 (32 ÷ 4 = 8). The rule of the sequence is to add 8 each time, so the missing numbers can now be worked out (5 + 8 = 13; 13 + 8 = 21; 21 + 8 = 29).

25 **195** To find *j*, divide the denominator by 4 and multiply the result by 3 (260 ÷ 4 = 65; 65 × 3 = 195).

26 **1.5** Find 20% as a fraction over 60 $\left(10\% = \frac{6}{60}\right.$ so $20\% = \frac{12}{60}\left.\right)$. This shows that $k + 10.5 = 12$, so subtract 10.5 from both sides to find that $k = 1.5$.

27 **502 cm²** Find the surface area by working out the areas of the three pairs of faces: top and bottom, right and left, and front and back. The top and bottom are each 104 cm² (8 cm × 13 cm = 104 cm²), giving a combined area of 208 cm². The right and left are 56 cm² each (8 cm × 7 cm = 56 cm²) for a combined area of 112 cm². The front and back are 91 cm² each (7 cm × 13 cm = 91 cm²) for a combined area of 182 cm². Add up the three amounts to find the total (208 cm² + 112 cm² + 182 cm² = 502 cm²).

28 **728 cm³** See Focus test 8, Q7.

29–31 The angles of a triangle total 180°, so subtracting the given angles from 180° will give the missing angle.

29 **94°** 180° − 43° − 43° = 94°

30 **18°** 180° − 108° − 54° = 18°

31 **23°** 180° − 90° − 67° = 23°

32 **24** Total sales are 42 ice creams + 38 drinks = 80 sales. The number of people who bought something was 56, so 80 sales − 56 people = 24 people who ordered both an ice cream and a drink.

33 **14** From the total of 38 people who ordered a drink, subtract the 24 people who ordered both an ice cream and a drink. This gives 14 people who ordered only a drink.

34 **144 seconds** Work out the multiples for each lighthouse, then find the lowest number that appears on all three lists. This is the lowest common multiple.
Sea Bass: 24, 48, 72, 96, 120, **144,** 168
White Bay: 18, 36, 54, 72, 90, 108, 126, **144**
Rock Ferry: 16, 32, 48, 64, 80, 96, 112, 128, **144**

35 **3:20 pm** Kishor walks at 3 miles an hour so 12 miles ÷ 3 = 4 hours required to complete his journey. He begins at 10:00 am, stops for lunch for 1 hour and takes breaks totalling 20 minutes, so he will finish his journey at 3:20 pm.

36 **2:20 pm** Haeon is walking at 4 miles an hour so 12 miles ÷ 4 = 3 hours required to complete his journey. He begins at 10:00 am, stops for lunch for 1 hour and takes breaks totalling 20 minutes, so he will finish his journey at 2:20pm.

37 **8.5m²** If 2 litres will cover 34 m², then 500 ml is $\frac{1}{4}$ of the amount of paint, so dividing the area by 4 will give the area that it will cover (34 m² ÷ 4 = 8.5 m²).

38 **11** Find the mean for Year 5 and Year 6 (See Focus test 12, Q2), then subtract the scores to find the difference. The mean for Year 5 is 65 (52 + 63 + 71 + 55 + 84 = 325; 325 ÷ 5 = 65) and the mean for Year 6 is 76 (63 + 76 + 82 + 67 + 92 = 380; 380 ÷ 5 = 76), so 76 − 65 = 11.

39 **76.5** See Mixed paper 2, Q48. The scores for Year 5 and Year 6 in English are 55, 67, **71, 82**, 84, 92 and 71 + 82 = 153; 153 ÷ 2 = 76.5.

40 **No** See Focus test 12, Q2. The new mean for Year 5 is 67 (52 + 63 + 68 + 71 + 55 + 84 = 402; 402 ÷ 6 = 67) and the new mean for Year 6 is 78 (63 + 76 + 88 + 82 + 67 + 92 = 468; 468 ÷ 6 = 78), so the difference remains the same (78 − 67 = 11).

41 **79** See Mixed paper 2, Q48. Year 6's results in order are now 63, 67, **76, 82**, 88, 92, so the new median is 79 (76 + 82 = 158; 158 ÷ 2 = 79).

42–44 **A (−1, 4), B (3, 4), C (3, −2)** When plotting coordinates on a grid, use the rule "along the corridor and up the stairs" to remember to go horizontal, then vertical.

45

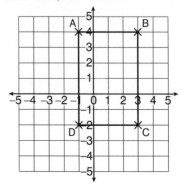

46 **(−1, −2)**

47 **5 days** The pie chart on the right represents the 30 days of June. The whole pie chart is 360°, so every 12° represents 1 day. The segment of 5–10 mm rain is 60°, so divide to find the number of days (360° ÷ 12° = 5 days).

48 $\frac{1}{3}$ There are 120° with less than 5 mm of rain. If 60° represents 5 days, then 120° represents 10 days. There are 30 days in June so this is $\frac{10}{30} = \frac{1}{3}$.

49 **No** Half of the days in each month had no rain but there are 28 days in February (in a non-leap year) and 30 days in June.

50 **21 days** There are 28 days in February, so half of those days had no rain, which is 14 days. A quarter of the days had less than 5 mm of rain, which is another 7 days. This is a total of 21 days.

Mixed Paper 10 (pages 60–63)

1–2 Work out the brackets first, then solve the remainder of the equation. Finally, divide the answer by the given amount.

1 **0.205** 42 ÷ 7 = 6; 6 + 14.5 = 20.5; 20.5 ÷ 100 = 0.205

2 **0.27** 11 × 24 = 264; 264 + 6 = 270; 270 ÷ 1000 = 0.27

3–5 **A = 22.3 kg, B = 34.5 kg, C = 18.05 kg** Take the total weight and subtract the sum of A + B to find C (74.85 kg − 56.8 kg = 18.05 kg). Then subtract the sum of B + C from the total weight to find A (74.85 kg − 52.55 kg = 22.3 kg). Now that A and C are known, subtract their weights from the total weight to find the weight of B (74.85 kg − 18.05 kg − 22.3 kg = 34.5 kg).

6 **18** Divide 3240 by 12 and then by 15 to find the missing number (3240 ÷ 12 = 270; 270 ÷ 15 = 18).

7–10

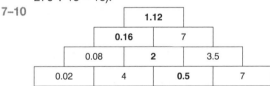

Divide 3.5 by 7 to find 0.5. Divide the other 7 by 3.5 to find 2. Multiply 2 by 0.08 to find 0.16, then multiply 0.16 by 7 to find 1.12.

11 **60**

12 **never** A square number always has an odd number of factors as one of the factor pairs is a single number multiplied by itself.

13 **41** See Mixed paper 1, Q14.

14 **2, 5, 17** Divide the number in order of prime factors until another prime number is left (170 ÷ 2 = 85; 85 ÷ 5 = 17).

15–18 $\frac{34}{85}$ < 0.46 < 65% < $\frac{42}{60}$ Make each value the same, using equivalent fractions ($\frac{34}{85} = \frac{2}{5} = \frac{40}{100}$; 65% = $\frac{65}{100}$; $\frac{42}{60} = \frac{7}{10} = \frac{70}{100}$; 0.46 = $\frac{46}{100}$). Then order them by size, starting with the smallest value.

19–21 See Focus test 4, Q5. Turn the flavours into a ratio (4 : 3 : 1) and add the numbers together to make a group (4 + 3 + 1 = 8) before working out how many groups are in the total number of sweets (32 ÷ 8 = 4). This shows that you can multiply each flavour by 4 to find the total number of each flavour.

19 **16** 4 × 4 = 16

20 **12** 4 × 3 = 12

21 **4** 4 × 1 = 4

22 **4n + 1** The first three rules work when the input number is 1: (1 × 1) + 4 = 5, (2 × 1) + 3 = 5, (4 × 1) + 1 = 5. The last rule does not and can be excluded. When the input number is 2, (1 × 2) + 4 = 6, (2 × 2) + 3 = 7, so that can be excluded. (4 × 1) + 1 = 5 and (4 × 2) + 1 = 9 so test it on the other input numbers: (4 × 3) + 1 = 13, (4 × 4) + 1 = 17, (4 × 5) + 1 = 21.

23 **41** To find the tenth number, use the rule and replace n with 10 (4 × 10 = 40; 40 + 1 = 41).

24–25 **0, −4.2** See Focus test 5, Q1. The rule for this sequence is to subtract 4.2 each time, so 4.2 − 4.2 = 0 and 0 − 4.2 = −4.2.

26–30 See Focus test 6, Q10–11.

26 **0.5** Subtract 1 from both sides to get rid of 1; this gives 5g = 2.5. Divide by 5 to find g (2.5 ÷ 5 = 0.5).

27 **3** Add 0.25 to both sides to get rid of −0.25; this gives $\frac{h}{4}$ = 0.75. Multiply both sides by 4 to find h (0.75 × 4 = 3).

28 **9** Divide by 7 to find p (63 ÷ 7 = 9).

29 **7** Multiply both terms in the brackets by 2 to find 104 − 6r = 62. Then add 6r to both sides to get rid of −6r; this gives 104 = 62 + 6r. Now subtract 62 from both sides to get rid of 62; this gives 42 = 6r. Divide by 6 to find r (42 ÷ 6 = 7).

30 **5** Multiply both terms in the brackets by 3 to find 12a + 6a = 90. Simplify this to find 18a = 90 and divide by 18 to find a (90 ÷ 18 = 5).

31 **false** A perpendicular line is at right angles to another line. Lines B and D are perpendicular.

32 **true** A parallel line runs in the same direction as another line, with the same distance between them all the way along, so they will never meet. No line is parallel to E.

33 **true** Lines B and G are perpendicular to D.

34 **true** Lines A and F are parallel.

35 **310.5 cm²** See Focus test 8, Q1. 23 cm × 13.5 cm = 310.5 cm²

36 **136 cm** See Focus test 8, Q2. 23 cm + 45 cm +

23 cm + 45 cm = 136 cm

37 **13972.5 cm³** See Focus test 8, Q7. 13.5 cm × 45 cm × 23 cm = 13972.5 cm³

38 **£600** There are 150 people going on the trip (140 + 10 = 150). Divide this by 34 seats per coach to find the number of coaches needed (150 ÷ 34 = 4.4). This shows that 5 coaches are needed, so multiply to find the total cost (5 × £120 = £600).

39 **£912.50** The total ticket cost for the adults is £125 (£12.50 × 10 = £125). There are 140 children and every tenth child is free, so divide by 10 to work out how many children go free (140 ÷ 10 = 14). Take this away from the total number of children to find out how many children to charge for (140 – 14 = 126). A child ticket is half the price of an adult ticket, so it costs £6.25 (£12.50 ÷ 2 = £6.25). For 126 children this will be £787.50 (126 × £6.25 = £787.50). Add the adult and child totals together to find the total ticket cost (£125 + £787.50 = £912.50).

40 **£10.00** Add the cost of travel to the ticket cost to find the total cost (£600 + £912.50 = £1512.50) and divide by the total number of people (£1512.50 ÷ 150 = £10.08 per person). That is closest to £10.00.

41 **1.19 km** If a runner covers 5 km in 42 minutes, then dividing the distance by the time gives the distance per minute (5 km ÷ 42 minutes = 0.119). Multiply this by 10 to show that the runner will have covered 1.19 km in 10 minutes. Alternatively, convert 5 km into 5000 m. 5000 ÷ 42 = approximately 119 m or 0.119 km per minute. Multiply this by 10.

42 **24 000 cm³** Convert all the measurements into centimetres – it is important to do this first. (300 mm ÷ 10 = 30 cm; 200 mm ÷ 10 = 20 cm; 400 mm ÷ 10 = 40 cm). Then multiply the three numbers to find the volume (30 cm × 20 cm × 40 cm = 24 000 cm³).

43–46 **(–4, 0) (–6, 1) (–4, 6) (–2, 5)**

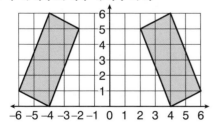

47 **2, 3** If the mean is 5, then the numbers on the cards must add up to 25 (5 cards × an average of 5 = 25). As the mode is 7, there are 2 cards showing a 7. The median, which is the middle number, is 6, so place these numbers in order (6, 7, 7) and add them together (6 + 7 + 7 = 20). The remaining two cards must add up to 5, so they could be 1 and 4 or 2 and 3. The range is 5 and the highest number is 7, so the lowest possible card is 2. This shows that the missing cards are 2 and 3.

48 $\frac{1}{4}$ There 12 pieces of fruit in the bag (4 + 5 + 3 = 12) and 3 of them are oranges, so $\frac{3}{12} = \frac{1}{4}$.

49 $\frac{1}{6}$ The chance of rolling a particular number on a single die is $\frac{1}{6}$. If there is a $\frac{1}{6}$ chance of rolling a 1 on the first die, and a $\frac{1}{6}$ chance of rolling a 1 on the second die, then multiply the two fractions to find the probability of rolling both together $\left(\frac{1}{6} \times \frac{1}{6} = \frac{1}{36}\right)$. There are 6 possible pairs of identical numbers, so $6 \times \frac{1}{36} = \frac{6}{36} = \frac{1}{6}$.

50 $\frac{1}{36}$ There is only one way to throw a total of 2 – by throwing a 1 on both die. There are 36 different possible combinations (6 × 6) so this is a 1 in 36 chance.

Bond Maths Assessment Papers Challenge 10–11+ years

NOTES

What is the difference in temperature between each pair of thermometers?

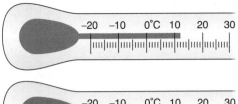

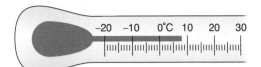

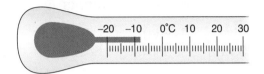

21 _____

22 _____

○ 2

23–24 Write the missing numbers in this sequence.

64　　81　　100　　_____　　144　　_____

○ 2

Work out the value of each letter.

25 $8v - 31 = 1$　　　　　　$v = $ _____

26 $3w + 9 = 27$　　　　　　$w = $ _____

27 $5q - 12 = 19 + 4$　　　　$q = $ _____

28 $8 + 7p = 6^2$　　　　　　$p = $ _____

29 $\dfrac{r}{10} = 5.6 - 4.8$　　　　$r = $ _____

○ 5

30 A square has an area of 625 cm². What is the length of each side?

_____

31 Calculate the area of a square with a perimeter of 18 m. _____

○ 2

What is the area of these triangles?

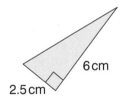

6 cm

2.5 cm

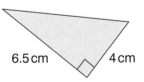

6.5 cm　　4 cm

32 area = _____　　**33** area = _____

○ 2

34 What is the height of a triangle if the area is 25.35 cm² and the base is 6.5 cm? _____ cm

○ 1

35 What is the base of a triangle if the area is 8.64 cm² and the height is 5.4 cm? _____ cm

○ 1

(33)

Circle the correct answer for each of these.

36 25% of 3 litres   1.25 litres   1500 ml   725 ml   0.75 litres

37 20% of 5.6 kg   1120 g   1.2 kg   11.2 kg   560 g   (2)

Look at the following measurements.

    4236 m   5.08 km   316 800 cm   4 938 000 mm
    4.235 km   5800 m   54 300 cm

38 What is the mean length in kilometres? _____

39 What is the median length in kilometres? _____

40 What is the range in kilometres? _____   (3)

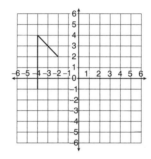

41 Mark the point (−2, −3) on the grid. This is the fourth corner of a quadrilateral. Draw two lines to complete this shape.

42 What is the name of this shape? _____

43–45 Rotate this shape 90° **clockwise** about the point (−2, −3). What are the coordinates of the other three corners of this rotated shape?

    (−2, −3) (__, __) (__, __) (__, __)   (5)

A teacher asked the class to sort a box of shapes. The children recorded the number of each shape on this bar graph.

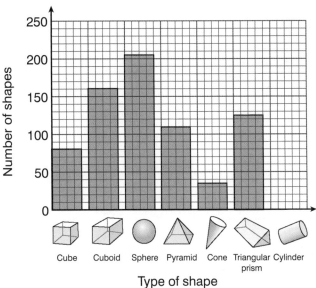

46 The children counted 85 cylinders. Accurately draw this bar on the graph.

47 Are there more shapes with 5 faces or 6 faces? _____

48 Which two shapes, when added together, have the same total as one other shape? _____

49 What percentage of the shapes are cuboids? _____

50 The teacher asked for all the shapes with a curved edge to be put into one box. How many shapes will there be in this box? _____

5

Now go to the Progress Chart to record your score!　Total　50

Mixed paper 4

Look at the table of diamonds and their uncut sizes.

Diamond	Uncut Size in mm
1 carat	6.048
3 carat	9.123
5 carat	11.845
7 carat	12.591
9 carat	13.514
15 carat	16.978

1 What size is the 1 carat diamond, rounded to the nearest hundredth?
_____

2 What size is the 9 carat diamond, rounded to the nearest whole number? _____

3 What size is the 15 carat diamond, rounded to the nearest tenth? _____   3

4 What is the value of the **5** in this number? 7.5882 _____   1

5 Multiply 33.764 by 10. _____   1

A stationery shop buys pencils in packets of 12. There are 16 packets in a box and there are 25 boxes to each container. Each container costs £1920.

6 If the stationers buy 1 container, how many pencils will they receive?
_____

7 How much will it cost them to buy each pencil? _____   2

The stationery shop buys pens for 35p each. The pens come in tubs of 14 and there are 15 tubs in each box. There are 18 boxes in a container. The stationers buy 2 containers.

8 How many pens are the stationers buying? _____

9 How much do they pay for 2 containers? _____   2

10   3288
            × 31
            _____

_____

36   1

Choose from the numbers 3, 5, 7 or 8 to complete these statements.

11–12 5166 is a multiple of _____ and _____.

13–14 2560 is a multiple of _____ and _____.

Ali, Kim and Dan each have a skipping rope. Dan's skipping rope is half the length of Kim's. Ali's skipping rope is $1\frac{1}{2}$ times longer than Kim's. The total length of their ropes when placed in a line end to end is 6m.

15 What is the length of Ali's skipping rope? _____

16 What is the length of Dan's skipping rope? _____

17 What is the length of Kim's skipping rope? _____

Convert these **improper fractions** to **mixed numbers** in their **lowest terms**.

18 $\dfrac{30}{9}$ _____ **19** $\dfrac{48}{10}$ _____

Simplify these expressions.

20 $3c + 2a^2 + a^2 - c =$ _____

21 $4(a-2) + 3a - 6 =$ _____

22 Solve y.

$4y + 7 = y + 13$

$y =$ _____

23 Solve x.

$15x - 12 = 5x + 3$

$x =$ _____

The rule for this sequence of numbers is: -200

4049   3849   3649   3449

What is the rule for each of these sequences?

24 6.4   4.2   2   −0.2   −2.4   rule: _____

25 $\dfrac{1}{2}$ $\dfrac{5}{8}$ $\dfrac{3}{4}$ $\dfrac{7}{8}$ 1   rule: _____

26–27 Work out the values of x and y in these triangles.

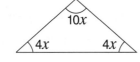

$x =$ _____ $y =$ _____

4

3

2

2

2

2

28 $\sqrt{d} = 12$ What is the value of d? _____

29 $\frac{r}{2} = 3$ What is the value of r? _____

○ 2

Look at this clock face and calculate the size of these angles. Do not use a protractor.

30 What is the size of the smaller angle between 12 and 4? _____

31 What is the size of the smaller angle between 8 and 9? _____

32 What is the angle between 5 and 11? _____

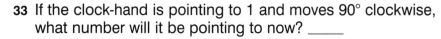

33 If the clock-hand is pointing to 1 and moves 90° clockwise, what number will it be pointing to now? _____

○ 4

Calculate the area of these triangles. Scale: each square represents 1 cm²

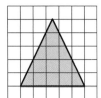
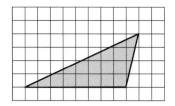

34 area = _____ **35** area = _____

○ 2

36 These are the dimensions of a cupboard.

What is the volume of the cupboard?

volume = _____

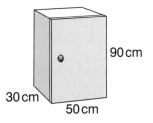

90 cm

30 cm

50 cm

○ 1

This net will fold to make a cuboid with square ends.

37 Calculate the total surface area of the cuboid. _____

38 Calculate the volume of the cuboid. _____

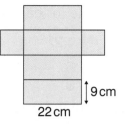

9 cm

22 cm

○ 2

39–40 The perimeter of a rectangular piece of paper is 900 mm. The length is 1.5 times the width. What is the length and width of this piece of paper?

Write your answers in centimetres.

length = _____ width = _____

○ 2

38

41–43 This biscuit recipe is out of an old cook book. Convert the ingredients from imperial units to metric units. Give your answers to the nearest 5g.

Use the approximation: 1 oz ≈ 28 g

Ingredient	Imperial	Metric
flour	14 oz	_____
butter	7 oz	_____
sugar	6 oz	_____

44 This recipe makes a total of eight biscuits. What is the weight of one biscuit? Give your answer in grams. _____

⚪ 4

Children from three classes recorded the number of pets owned. They displayed the data on these pie charts.

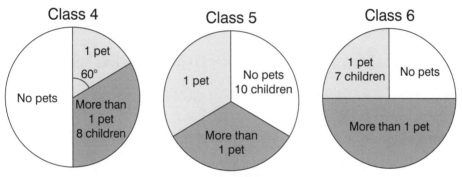

45–47 How many children are there in each class?

Class 4 _____ children

Class 5 _____ children

Class 6 _____ children

48 How many children in total from all three classes have only one pet? _____

49 How many more children have no pets in Class 4 than those with no pets in Class 6? _____

50 Is this statement 'true', 'false' or is it 'impossible to say'? Circle the answer.

The same number of children in Class 4 and Class 5 have more than one pet.

        true   false   impossible to say

⚪ 6

Mixed paper 5

Write these numbers on the answer lines to make this statement true.

2.09   0.927   0.279   2.7

1–4 ____ < ____ < ____ < ____   4

5 I'm thinking of a number less than 1. The two digits total 9 and it rounds to 0.4 to the nearest tenth.

What is the number I am thinking of? 0. __ __   1

6 A piece of wood is 189cm long. It is cut into six equal lengths.

How long is each length? _____   1

7 (378 ÷ 18) + 19 = ____   **8** (403 ÷ 13) + 15 = ____   2

9 A 2 litre bottle of lemonade is poured into 0.4 litre glasses.

How many glasses will be filled? ____

10 Joe saves the same amount each week. After 20 weeks he has saved £75.

How much does he save each week? _____   2

Circle the number in each row that has each pair of numbers as factors.

11 4 and 7   8   14   27   28   32

12 13 and 3   9   19   31   33   39   2

13 Circle the number that has five factors.

12   14   16   18   1

14–15 Two of these numbers are multiples of 4, 7 and 9. Circle them.

588   126   756   252   576   2

16 What is the ratio of spheres to cubes on this necklace? _____

17 A longer necklace is made with the same pattern. If 15 spherical beads are used, how many cubed beads will be needed? ____   2

Change these fractions into decimals.

18 $\frac{24}{30}$ = _____   **19** $\frac{28}{70}$ = _____   ◯ 2

20 In a sale a coat is reduced by 40% from the original price of £125.

What is the new price of the coat in the sale? _____

21 In a sale a book is reduced by 15% from the original price of £25.

What is the new price of the book in the sale? _____

22 In a sale a game has been reduced by 20% and now costs £40.

What was the original price of the game? _____   ◯ 3

23 What is the cube root of 729? _____   ◯ 1

Leroy has made this pattern from colouring in squares on a grid.

The table shows the number of squares he coloured each time.

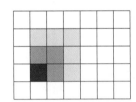

Shape	1	2	3	4	n
Squares	1	3	5	___	?

24 How many squares will he colour for the 4th shape? Write your answer in the table.

25 What is the correct formula for this pattern? Circle the answer.

$n + 3$ $4n - 1$ $3n + 1$ $n + 4$ $2n - 1$

26 Leroy continues with this pattern. How many squares will he colour in the 8th shape? _____   ◯ 3

What is the value of each of these letters?

27 $17 + 8e = 73$ $e =$ _____

28 $4f + (27 \div 9) = 35$ $f =$ _____   ◯ 2

A clock has the big hand on 12 and the small hand moves clockwise. What time is it when the angle between the two hands has these values?

29 180° _____o'clock   **30** 30° _____o'clock   **31** 150° _____o'clock   ◯ 3

(41)

32 What is the area of a rectangular car park that is 8.4 m wide and 15 m long? _____

1

Calculate the area of these shapes.

33 area = _____

34 area = _____

2

35 A cuboid has a square base of 36 cm². The volume of the cuboid is 5292 cm³.

What is the height of the cuboid? _____

1

Cat food comes in a bag weighing 5.5 kg. The bag states that cats should be fed 30 g of food daily for every 500 g the cat weighs.

36 Top Cat is 4 kg in weight. How much food will he eat in a week?

_____

37 Princess is 6 kg in weight. Roughly how many weeks would a bag of food last her? _____

38 Zizi eats 1 bag every 4 weeks. How much food does she eat in a year, in kilograms? _____

39 Catkin, who eats 1700 g each week, wins a year's supply of cat food as a prize in a cat show. How many bags of food would it take to feed him for a year, to the nearest whole bag? _____

4

At the supermarket there are different size boxes of the same cereal.

40 Which box of cereal is the best value? _____

41 Which box of cereal is the worst value? _____

2

42 Rotate line A 90° **clockwise** about the point (−4, −3). Draw the new line and label it B.

Complete the coordinates of line B.
(−4, −3) and (__, __)

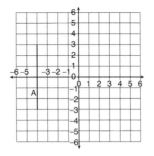

43 Is line B **parallel** or **perpendicular**

to Line A? _____

44 Lines A and B are two sides of a square.

What are the coordinates of the missing corner of this square? (__, __) ◯ 3

45 This is an isosceles triangle. Write in the missing coordinates.

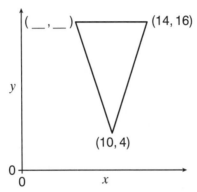

◯ 1

These are the number of pages six children read in half an hour.

28   33   27   19   25   24

46 What is the range? _____   **47** What is the mean? _____   ◯ 2

48 There is a $\frac{1}{5}$ chance of picking a raffle ticket that will win a prize. What is the probability of picking a raffle ticket that will not win a prize?

_____

◯ 1

There are 60 beads in a box: 12 are red, 18 are blue, 20 are green and the rest are yellow.

49 What is the chance of taking out a bead that is not yellow? Circle the answer.

$\frac{1}{2}$ $\frac{2}{3}$ $\frac{3}{4}$ $\frac{5}{6}$ $\frac{11}{12}$

50 What is the chance of taking out a blue bead? Circle the answer.

$\frac{1}{3}$ $\frac{3}{10}$ $\frac{3}{6}$ $\frac{1}{10}$ $\frac{3}{4}$

◯ 2

Mixed paper 6

Write the missing sign: $\times$ or $\div$

1　14.25 ___ 10 = 142.5

2　0.587 ___ 100 = 58.7

3　6.03 ___ 10 = 0.603

4–5　Choose any two of the digits below to make the statement on the right correct.

　　7.2　　3.4　　6.8　　3.2　　9.7　　　　　___ $\times$ ___ = 21.76

6　6 $\div$ 0.4 = ___

7　7.2 $\div$ 8 = ___

Class 6 hold up all of the digits from 0 to 9 and a decimal point. They then stand in a different, random order 5 times to make 5 different numbers. Here are the numbers they made.

Order	Number Made
1	62 497.3108
2	961.287543
3	786 954.123
4	5 139 768.24
5	1324.57698

8　What number is Order 1 to the nearest hundred? ___

9　What number is Order 5 to the nearest thousandth? ___

10　What number is Order 4 to the nearest thousand? ___

11　Write **always**, **sometimes** or **never** to make this statement true.

　　A square number ___ has an odd number of factors.

Look at this set of numbers.

　　　　　80　　81　　82　　83　　84　　85

12　Which is a prime number? ___　13　Which is a square number? ___

44

14 Which is a multiple of 2 and 3? _____

15 A model village is made to a scale of 2 cm to every 3 metres.
A real tree is 12 m tall.

What is the height of the model tree? _____

Circle the smallest value in each set.

16 $\frac{5}{8}$ of 24 $\frac{2}{3}$ of 18 $\frac{2}{5}$ of 25 $\frac{3}{7}$ of 21

17 0.27   0.07   0.2   0.72

18 $\frac{40}{56}$ $\frac{8}{14}$ $\frac{27}{63}$ $\frac{42}{49}$

19 Write < or > to make this statement true.   2% ___ 0.2

Add <, > or = to make these statements correct.

20 $4^2 \times 3^2$ _____ $12^2 \div 1^2$ **21** $5^3 + 11^2$ _____ $8^2 \times 2^2$

22 $\sqrt{100} + 33 =$ _____

23 Which two square numbers total 80? _____ and _____

24 Circle the formula for the **area** of this triangle.

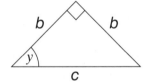

$2(b \times c)$ $(b \times b) \div 2$ $2(b \times b)$ $(2 \times c) \div b$

25 Circle the formula for the **perimeter** of this triangle.

$b + c$ $2b - c$ $b - c$ $2b + c$ $2b + 2c$

26 Circle the name of this type of triangle.

isosceles   equilateral   scalene

27 Calculate the size of angle y in this triangle. _____

28 How many diagonal lines can be drawn in the pentagon below? _____

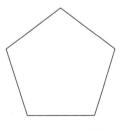

(Right margin mark boxes: 1, 1, 3, 1, 2, 2, 4, 1)

29–32 Write the missing information in this table.

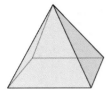 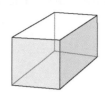 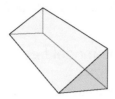 

Shape name	Number of faces	Number of corners	Number of edges
tetrahedron	___	4	6
cuboid	6	8	___
square-based pyramid	5	___	8
triangular prism	5	6	___

33 Which net will **not** fold to make a closed cube? _____

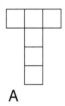   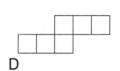

A   B   C   D

34 Draw three more lines to make a parallelogram with an area of 12 squares.

The top of this table has a surface area of 3200 cm². The length of the table-top is double the width.

35–36 What is the length and width of the table-top?

length = _____   width = _____

37 The tablecloth hangs over the edge of the table by 15 cm all the way round.

What is the area of the tablecloth? _____

This shows the area of each face of a cuboid.

38 What is the volume of the cuboid? _____

4

1

1

3

1

39 Circle the name of this type of triangle.

equilateral   isosceles   scalene
right-angled

40 How many lines of symmetry are there on this triangle? _____

41–43 Draw another triangle using these coordinates: (0, 3), (2, 9) and (4, 3)

44 Is this triangle a translation, rotation or reflection of the first triangle?

_____

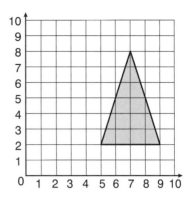

6

Distance conversion (kilometres to miles)

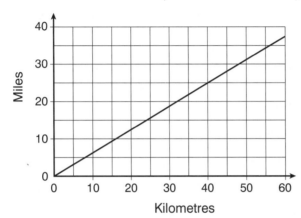

45–47 Use this conversion graph to convert these distances.

16 km: _____ miles (to the nearest whole mile)

28 miles: _____ kilometres (to the nearest whole km)

23 miles: _____ kilometres (to the nearest whole km)

48 Which is the further distance? 20 miles or 30 km _____

49 A lorry only has enough fuel to drive 15 miles. A sign shows that the filling station is in 22 km. Does the lorry have enough fuel to get to the filling station? Circle the answer.   Yes   No

50 The speed on my car is shown in miles per hour (mph). I am travelling in France and the speed limit is 50 km per hour (kph). What is the fastest speed I can drive my car and not go over the 50 kph speed limit? Give the answer to the nearest 10 mph. _____ mph

6

Mixed paper 7

Round each number to the nearest tenth.

1 0.71 _____   2 2.35 _____

3 10.164 _____   4 96.48 _____   ○ 4

5 A wall is 100 bricks high and each brick is 0.08m high.

What is the height of the wall? _____   ○ 1

6 What is the product of 384 and 23? _____   ○ 1

7 If six plates cost £8.40, how much would eight plates cost? _____   ○ 1

8–10 The product of three numbers is 133650. The first number is a 2-digit number less than 50 with digits that are consecutive numbers. The second number is a 2-digit number which has the same digits as the first number reversed and is greater than 40. The third number is a 2-digit number that has the same number for both digits and can be found in the 5 times table.

What are the three numbers? _____ _____ _____   ○ 3

11–15 Write these numbers on the Venn diagram:

24   36   54   86   104   ○ 5

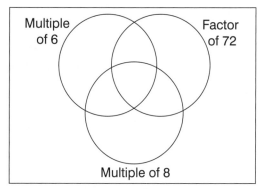

Jet has a 1.5 kg pizza that is divided into 8 equal pieces. Esosa has a 750g pizza that is divided into 5 equal pieces.

16 If Jet eats 2 pieces of his pizza and Esosa eats 3 pieces of her pizza, how much do they each eat? Jet = _____   Esosa = _____

17 If Jet eats one more slice, who has eaten more pizza? _____   ○ 2

Change these fractions into percentages.

18 $\dfrac{24}{96}$ = _____   19 $\dfrac{45}{150}$ = _____   ○ 2

48

20 On a school watersports trip there must be a ratio of 2 adults to every 5 children. Class 4H has 32 children and Class 4K has 28 children.

How many adults are needed? _____

21–22 Write the missing numbers.

$$\underline{}^2 + \underline{}^2 = 5^2$$

Write the missing numbers in these sequences.

23 1000   729   512   _____   216   125   64

24 _____   196   144   100   64   36   16

Use l for the length and w for width to answer these questions.

w

l

25 Circle the formula for the **perimeter** of this rectangle.

$$4(w + l) \qquad \tfrac{1}{2}(w + l) \qquad 2(w + l) \qquad w(2 + l)$$

26 This equation shows the area of a rectangle. Calculate the length, l, of the rectangle.

$$345\,\text{cm}^2 = l \times 15\,\text{cm} \qquad l = \underline{}$$

Write the value of each letter in these equations.

27 $4m^2 = 64$ $m = \underline{}$

28 $3n^2 = 108$ $n = \underline{}$

29 $4c^2 - 15 = 85$ $c = \underline{}$

Write the name of the solid shape that can be made from each net.

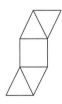

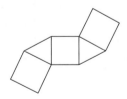

30 _____   **31** _____

32 The dashed line is a mirror line. Draw the reflected shape.

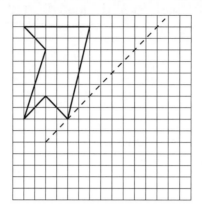

1

33–35 Calculate the angle marked with the letter in each shape.

Shape 1 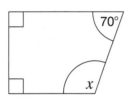 Shape 2 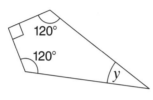 Shape 3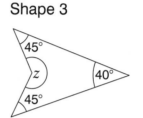

angle x = _____   angle y = _____   angle z = _____

3

36–39 Complete the following chart.

Gift box shape	Length of lid	Width of lid	Area of lid	Height of box	Volume of box
cube	_____	17 cm	289 cm²	17 cm	_____
cuboid	9.5 cm	8 cm	_____	_____	8740 cm³

4

40 Calculate the total area of this windmill.

_____

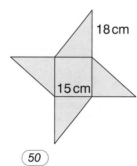

18 cm

15 cm

1

50

41 What must be added to 405g to make 1.56kg? Write your answer in kilograms. _____

◯ 1

42 Circle the longer length.

50cm   50 inches

◯ 1

Give each answer in the unit of measurement shown.

43 12.6kg ÷ 9 = _____ g

44 44m ÷ 8 = _____ cm

◯ 2

This graph shows the time it took two walkers to complete a 30 km walk.

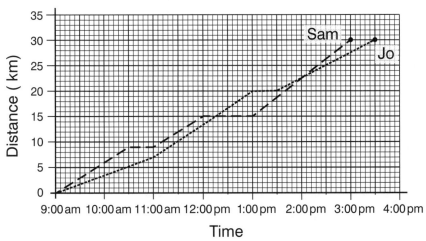

30km sponsored walk

45 How far had Sam walked by 10:30am? _____

46 Who finished their walk first, Sam or Jo? _____

47 How long did Sam stop for rests in total? _____

48 How much further had Sam walked than Jo at 11:00am?

_____

49 Sam was sitting eating lunch when Jo walked past. Approximately what time was this? _____

50 What was Jo's average speed for the 30km walk, not including rest time? _____ km per hour

◯ 6

Round each of these numbers to the nearest whole number.

1 491.3 _____   **2** 27.449 _____   **3** 50.52 _____   ◯ 3

4–5 The secret code to unlock a padlock has 6 digits made from 3 double-digit numbers. The first double-digit number is between 10 and 18. The second double-digit number is the first double-digit number multiplied by 2. The third double-digit number is the first double-digit number multiplied by 3. The secret code has NO digits of the same value.

What is the code? _____   ◯ 2

6 A chicken farmer collects 760 eggs in one day. An egg carton holds 12 eggs.

How many full cartons will there be and how many eggs are left over?

_____ full cartons   _____ eggs left over   ◯ 1

7 By how much is the product of 15 and 29 greater than their sum?

_____   ◯ 1

Anupama has arranged the digits 1, 2 and 5 to make 6 different 3-digit numbers.

8 Which two numbers are prime numbers? _____ _____

9 Which number is a cube number? _____

10 Which number has the factors 1, 2, 4, 8, 19, 38, 76 and itself? _____   ◯ 3

11 What is the **highest common factor** of 18 and 45? _____

12–13 Circle the **prime factors** of 18.

2   3   4   5   6   7   8   9

14–15 Multiply the highest common factor of 24 and 36 by the lowest common multiple of 4 and 5. _____   ◯ 5

Five biscuits are made from 75g of flour, 50g of butter and 25g of sugar.

16 How much will each biscuit weigh? _____

17 What proportion of the biscuit is sugar? Circle the answer.   ◯ 2

$$\frac{1}{2} \qquad \frac{1}{4} \qquad \frac{1}{5} \qquad \frac{1}{6}$$

18 How much butter is needed if 300g of flour is used?_____

19 What is the ratio of flour to butter in this recipe? Circle the answer.

$$1:1 \qquad 2:1 \qquad 3:2 \qquad 6:1 \qquad 7:5$$

○ 2

Look at this set of numbers.

21   29   39   49   51

20 Which number is a square number? _____

21 Which number is a prime number? _____

○ 2

22 The temperature on a thermometer at midday was 11°C. The thermometer was read again at midnight and the temperature had dropped by 14°C.

What was the temperature at midnight? _____

○ 1

Write the next number in each sequence.

23 1   1   2   3   5   8   _____

24 36864   18432   9216   4608   _____

25 3000   300   30   3   _____

○ 3

Use l for the length and w for width to answer these questions.

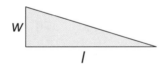

26 Circle the formula for the **area** of this triangle.

$$2(l \times w) \qquad (l \times w) \div 2 \qquad (l \times w) + 2 \qquad 2(w \div l)$$

27 Calculate the area of this triangle, when w = 4cm and l = 15cm. _____

○ 2

If s = 8 and t = 9, what is the value of each of these equations?

28 $(7s - 11) \div t =$ _____

29 $t^2 - (s + 13) =$ _____

30 $16t \div s =$ _____

○ 3

31 A shape has 5 faces, 6 vertices and 9 edges.

What is the name of this shape? _____

32 The net of a shape has one pentagon and five triangles.

What is the name of this shape?

_____

33 Name the solid shape that
can be made from this net.

_____

_____

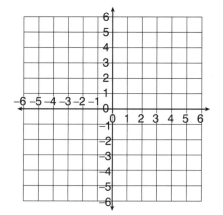

34 A regular hexagon has sides 14mm long.

What is the perimeter of this hexagon in centimetres? _____cm

35 Add together 585ml, 3.2 litres and 1 litre 75ml. Write your answer in litres. _____

36 Circle the greater length.   9 metres   9 feet

Give each answer in the unit of measurement shown.

37 470cm + 3062mm + 1.603m = _____mm

38 51cm + 51mm + 51m = _____cm

39 879cm + 400mm + 9.4m = _____m

40–43 Plot these coordinates and join them
in order to make a quadrilateral.
Label each point with its letter. Draw
a line from point D to point A to
complete the shape.

A (1, 3)   B (−2, 6)

C (−5, 3)   D (−2, −5)

44 What is the name of this shape?

_____

3

1

1

1

3

5

54

These 10 cards were placed in a bag and selected randomly.

| 10 | 20 | 30 | 40 | 50 | 60 | 70 | 80 | 90 | 100 |

For each question, write the probability as a decimal. Use this scale to help you.

Impossible   Certain
0   0.5   1

45 What is the probability of picking a number that is greater than 35? _____

46 What is the probability of picking a square number? _____

47 What is the probability of picking an odd number? _____

48 What is the probability of picking a multiple of 3? _____

49 What is the probability of picking an even number? _____

50 What is the probability of picking a multiple of 4? _____   6

Now go to the Progress Chart to record your score!   Total   50

Mixed paper 9

These are the times for the medallists in the women's 50 m freestyle swimming final in the 2004 Olympics.

Swimmer	Time (seconds)
Libby Lenton, Australia	24.91
Inge De Bruijn, Netherlands	24.58
Malia Metella, France	24.89

1 What was the winning time?

___ ___ • ___ ___ seconds

Divide each number by 100 to give the **quotient**.

2 703.16 _____

3 59.4 _____

Use these four digits and the decimal point to answer both questions.

> 3　8　0　5　•

4 What is the largest possible number?　___ • ___ ___ ___

5 What is the smallest possible number?　___ • ___ ___ ___

6 The product of two numbers is 1083. One of the numbers is 57.

What is the other number? _____

7 Which number, when multiplied by 45, will give the same answer as

7.2×100? _____

8 Five cinema tickets cost a total of £22.25. The tickets were all the same price.

How much was one ticket? _____

9–10 Write the missing digits in this calculation.

3__2 × 24 = 844__

11–14 Write these numbers on the Carroll diagram.　**147**　**121**　**49**　**128**

	Square number	Not a square number
Multiple of 7	_____	_____
Not a multiple of 7	_____	_____

56

Change these fractions into percentages.

15 $\dfrac{42}{210}$ = _____

16 $\dfrac{68}{80}$ = _____

Class 3 recorded the number of each type of vehicle passing the school.

Cars	Bikes	Lorries	Buses
144	36	48	12

17 What percentage of vehicles were cars? _____

18 What fraction of vehicles were lorries? Express the fraction in its lowest terms. _____

19 What percentage of vehicles were buses? _____

20 Out of the Bikes group, 27 were bicycles. What fraction of the Bikes group were bicycles? Express the fraction in its lowest terms. _____

21 Write < or > to make the following true. $\sqrt{36}$ ___ 6.3

22–24 In this sequence the same amount is added each time. Write the missing numbers.

5   ___   ___   ___   37

Write the value of each letter in these equations.

25 $\dfrac{j}{260} = \dfrac{3}{4}$ $j =$ ___

26 $\dfrac{k + 10.5}{60} = 20\%$ $k =$ ___

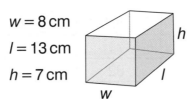

$w = 8\,cm$
$l = 13\,cm$
$h = 7\,cm$

27 What is the surface area of this shape? _____

28 Calculate the volume of this shape. _____

Work out the value of the angles x, y and z in these triangles.

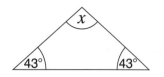 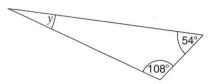 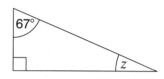

29 $x =$ _____   **30** $y =$ _____   **31** $z =$ _____   ⬤ 3

At an ice cream stall, there are 56 people who bought either an ice cream or a drink or both. 42 people ordered an ice cream. 38 people ordered a drink. Some people ordered an ice cream and a drink.

32 How many people ordered both an ice cream and a drink? _____

33 How many people ordered a drink, but not an ice cream? _____   ⬤ 2

34 The Sea Bass Lighthouse flashes every 24 seconds. The White Bay Lighthouse flashes every 18 seconds. The Rock Ferry Lighthouse flashes every 16 seconds. If they all flash together, after how many seconds will they all flash together again? _____   ⬤ 1

Kishor and Haeon are each walking a journey of 12 miles. Kishor is walking at 3 miles an hour and Haeon is walking at 4 miles an hour. They both set out at 10:00 am and stop for lunch at 12:00 pm for one hour, plus 2 breaks of 10 minutes each.

35 At what time will Kishor complete his walk? _____

36 At what time will Haeon complete his walk? _____   ⬤ 2

37 2 litres of paint will cover an area of 34 m².

What area can be covered by 500 ml of paint? _____   ⬤ 1

Look at the following table of maths and English test results for Year 5 and Year 6.

	Maths 1	Maths 2	English 1	English 2	English 3
Year 5	52	63	71	55	84
Year 6	63	76	82	67	92

38 What was the difference between the mean score for Year 5 and the mean score for Year 6? _____

39 What was the median for all of the English results? _____

58

40–41 A third maths test takes place: Year 5 scores 68 and Year 6 scores 88. Has the difference in mean between Year 5 and Year 6 changed?

_____

What is the new median for the total results for Year 6? _____ (4)

42–44 What are the coordinates of points A, B and C?

A (__, __)   B (__, __)   C (__, __)

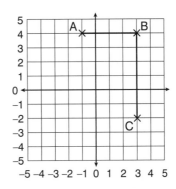

Lines AB and BC are two sides of a rectangle.

45 Mark the position of the fourth vertex and complete the rectangle.

46 What are the coordinates of the fourth vertex of the rectangle? (__, __) (5)

These two pie charts show the number of days it rained in February and June. It was not a leap year.

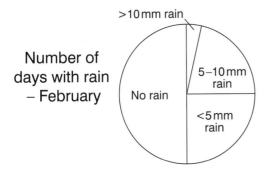

Number of days with rain – February

Number of days with rain – June

47 How many days in June had 5–10 mm of rain? _____

48 What fraction of the days in June had less than 5 mm rain? _____

49 Sam says, "There were the same number of days in February and in June that had no rain." Is Sam correct? _____

50 How many days in February had either no rain or less than 5 mm of rain? _____ (4)

1 (42 ÷ 7) + 14.5   What is the answer divided by 100? _____

2 (11 × 24) + 6   What is the answer divided by 1000? _____   ◯ 2

3–5 Parcels A, B and C weigh 74.85 kg.

   Parcel A + Parcel B = 56.8 kg.

   Parcel B + Parcel C = 52.55 kg.

   How heavy is each parcel?

   A = _____   B = _____   C = _____   ◯ 3

6 Three whole numbers multiplied together total 3240. Two of the
   numbers are 12 and 15. What is the third number? _____   ◯ 1

7–10 Complete the following pyramid. Each pair of numbers on the bottom
   row are multiplied together to find the number on the row above.

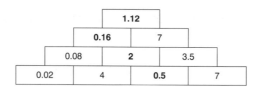

◯ 4

11 What is the lowest common multiple of 10 and 12? _____   ◯ 1

12 Write **always**, **sometimes** or **never** to make this statement true.

   A square number will _____ have an even number of factors.

13 Write the next number in this sequence of consecutive prime numbers.

   23   29   31   37   ___

14 Which three prime numbers multiply to make 170? ___, ___, ___   ◯ 3

15–18 Put these values in order, starting with the smallest.

$$\frac{34}{85} \qquad 65\% \qquad \frac{42}{60} \qquad 0.46$$

   ___ < ___ < ___ < ___   ◯ 4

There are three different flavoured sweets in a packet. There are 4 cherry to 3 lemon to 1 mint. There are 32 sweets in a pack. Calculate the number of each flavour sweet.

19 cherry: _____ **20** lemon: _____ **21** mint: _____ ◯ 3

Look at the machine below.

IN	1	2	3	4	5
OUT	5	9	13	17	21

22 What is the rule for this machine? Circle the correct answer.

1n + 4   2n + 3   4n + 1   4n − 4

23 If the sequence of inputs were continued, what number would appear in the 'OUT' row for the tenth number in the sequence? _____ ◯ 2

24–25 Write the next two numbers in this sequence.

16.8   12.6   8.4   4.2   _____   _____ ◯ 2

What number does each letter represent?

26 $5g + 1 = 3.5$ $g =$ ___   **27** $\frac{h}{4} - 0.25 = 0.5$ $h =$ ___

28 $7p = 63$ $p =$ ___   **29** $(52 - 3r) \times 2 = 62$ $r =$ ___

30 $3(4a + 2a) = 90$ $a =$ ___ ◯ 5

Look at these lines. Circle **true** or **false** for each statement.

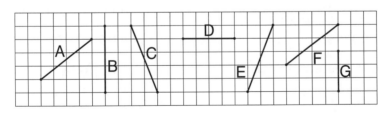

31 There is no line perpendicular to B.   **true**   **false**

32 There is no line parallel to E.   **true**   **false**

33 There are two lines perpendicular to D.   **true**   **false**

34 Lines A and F are parallel.   **true**   **false** ◯ 4

Look at this cuboid.

35 What is the area of face A? _____

36 What is the perimeter of face C? _____

37 What is the volume of the cuboid?

_____

C   13.5 cm
B
A   45 cm
23 cm

3

There are 140 children and 10 adults going on a school trip to a castle. The cost of a coach for the day is £120 and the coach will seat 34 people. The ticket for the castle is £12.50 for adults and half price for children, but for every 10 children, 1 of the tickets is free.

38 What is the total cost of travel? _____

39 What is the total cost for the tickets? _____

40 To the nearest pound, what is the total cost of travel plus tickets, divided equally between everyone? _____

41 A runner completes a 5 km race in 42 minutes. He runs at the same pace for the whole distance.

How many metres has he run after 10 minutes? Write your answer in kilometres to 2 decimal places. _____ km

42 A coolbox is 300 mm high, 200 mm wide and 400 mm deep.

What is the volume of the coolbox in cubic centimetres?

_____ cm^3

3

1

1

Reflect this rectangle into the second quadrant and plot the points.

43–46 What are the coordinates of your rectangle?

(__, __) (__, __) (__, __) (__, __)

6
5
4
3
2
1
0
-6 -5 -4 -3 -2 -1 0 1 2 3 4 5 6

4

47 Five cards are chosen from two sets of 1–10 number cards. The median is 6, the mode is 7, the mean is 5 and the range is 5.

What are the two lowest numbers on the cards? __ and __

1

48 There are 4 apples, 5 pears and 3 oranges in a bag. What is the probability of picking out an orange? Circle the answer.

$$\frac{2}{3} \qquad \frac{1}{2} \qquad \frac{1}{3} \qquad \frac{3}{4} \qquad \frac{1}{4}$$

○ 1

Solomon rolls two fair, 6-numbered dice and records the total score. He rolls the dice 10 times.

49 What is the probability of Solomon scoring the same number on each dice? _____

50 What is the probability that he will record a total score of 2? _____

○ 2

Now go to the Progress Chart to record your score!   Total ○ 50